THE
ADVENTURE
of
DISCIPLING
OTHERS

Training in the Art of Disciplemaking

RON BENNETT AND JOHN PURVIS

NAVPRESS

Discipleship Inside Out™

NAVPRESS
Discipleship Inside Out™

NavPress is the publishing ministry of The Navigators, an international Christian organization and leader in personal spiritual development. NavPress is committed to helping people grow spiritually and enjoy lives of meaning and hope through personal and group resources that are biblically rooted, culturally relevant, and highly practical.

For a free catalog go to www.NavPress.com
or call 1.800.366.7788 in the United States or 1.800.839.4769 in Canada.

The Navigators Church Discipleship Ministry (CDM) is focused on helping churches become more intentional in disciplemaking. CDM staff nationwide are available to help church leadership develop the critical components that will enable them to accomplish Christ's Great Commission. For further information on how CDM can help you, contact our office at 719-594-2446.

ISBN 978-1-57683-348-3

Cover design by Arvid Wallen
Creative Team: Paul Santhouse, Brad Lewis, Amy Spencer, Pat Reinheimer

Some of the anecdotal illustrations in this book are true to life and are included with the permission of the persons involved. All other illustrations are composites of real situations, and any resemblance to people living or dead is coincidental.

Unless otherwise identified, all Scripture quotations in this publication are taken from the HOLY BIBLE: NEW INTERNATIONAL VERSION® (NIV®). Copyright © 1973, 1978, 1984 by International Bible Society. Used by permission of Zondervan Publishing House. All rights reserved. Other versions used include the *New American Standard Bible* (NASB), © The Lockman Foundation 1960, 1962, 1963, 1968, 1971, 1972, 1973, 1975, 1977; and *The Message: New Testament with Psalms and Proverbs* (MSG) by Eugene H. Peterson, copyright © 1993, 1994, 1995, used by permission of NavPress Publishing Group.

Printed in the United States of America

8 9 10 11 12 / 18 17 16 15 14

For further information regarding this material and other discipling resources contact:

CDM™
CHURCH DISCIPLESHIP MINISTRY

The Navigators
P.O. Box 6000
Colorado Springs, CO 80934
www.navigators.org/cdm

CONTENTS

PREFACE

WELCOME TO THE EXCITING, challenging, and fulfilling ministry of discipling others. Maybe you're considering this kind of ministry for the first time or maybe you're a seasoned veteran. Perhaps you're looking for help getting started or for resources to keep you going. Whatever your level of disciplemaking experience, we hope this material will help you develop greater heart, vision, and skill in your journey.

We've designed this material for use with a cluster group, preferably with a discipling coach or mentor leading the group. This material can supplement the experience and teaching of the coach as he or she guides the group in learning how to disciple others.

If you don't have a coach, we encourage you to work through this material with a group of fellow learners. Rotate facilitating the leadership for the various sessions. You'll experience great benefits by forming a small group or team of disciplers to share and learn together and from each other. If you can't form a cluster group, you can still work through this material on your own. Obviously, some of the activities built around small-group dynamics won't apply. But you can still work through the Bible studies and articles as you're involved in discipling others.

The Adventure of Discipling Others is designed to be used simultaneously with the actual experience of discipling at least one other person. Learning by doing is critical to making this material authentic rather than academic. There's no substitute to stepping out and investing your life in someone else's life. Such faith pleases God, and His resources are always adequate.

As you get involved in discipling others, be aware that growing disciples aren't all starting at the same point. Some will be brand-new believers; others will be Christians looking for more depth in their walk with Christ. Therefore, no one set of materials will fit everyone. You'll have to decide what material fits your situation. We've included some suggestions in appendix A, Discipling Resources (page 216), but there is a great deal of other material on the market that you can choose from. Your church, pastor, or discipling coach is probably a good source for additional ideas.

When discipling others, use what's meaningful to you. If you've been discipled with certain materials, that should be the starting point for choosing the material you pass on to others. If you don't have experience with specific materials, be sure to work through any new material you choose before you use it with others.

INTRODUCTION

OVERVIEW

THE ADVENTURE OF DISCIPLING OTHERS is a flexible resource that will equip disciples to disciple other people. The goal of this material is to contribute to the development of spiritual generations through a life-to-life ministry of discipling. It will help a third generation of disciples to emerge that is central to an intentional disciplemaking community. Once these people become established, they'll have the heart, vision, and skill to intentionally disciple others whether the context is a small group or individual. (If you're not familiar with some of these terms, you'll learn more about them as you read on.)

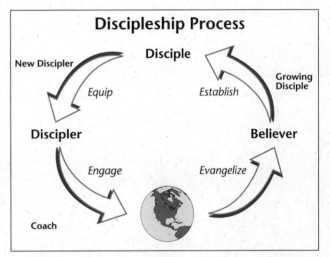

In the illustration at right, the first person in this process is the new discipler. New disciplers are the link to a new generation of disciples as they seek to pass on to others what they've discovered in their walk of faith. The new discipler is critical in developing a spiritual heritage that reproduces.

The second person in the triad is the new believer. New believers who are becoming mature disciples are the new generation. They're growing in their relationship to Christ as disciples in the context of a supportive community. Each person at this stage of maturity is establishing a personal faith relationship with Christ that is foundational, lifelong, and intimate.

The third person in this triad is the coach—the one who assists the new discipler as he or she disciples others. A coach in this concept of generations is much like a grandparent in a physical family. He or she is primarily focused on helping the discipler be successful. The coach, discipler, and growing disciple form a spiritual unity promoted in Paul's ministry through Timothy (see 2 Timothy 2:2).

The hope for this triad is that it will develop future generations of mature believers. As the growing disciple experiences the reality of a changed life through the model of the discipler, he or she will become a new discipler (new spiritual parent). This process develops an ongoing spiritual lineage that can reach the world. No one should be the last link in a spiritual chain.

DEFINITIONS

We use the following working definitions throughout *The Adventure of Discipling Others:*

- *Believer*—someone who has come to personal faith in Jesus Christ
- *Growing disciple*—a believer who wants to mature as a disciple and is becoming established in his or her faith through the exercise of spiritual disciplines
- *Disciple*—an individual who has received foundational training and has become established in the principles and practices of following Christ
- *New discipler*—a disciple of Jesus Christ who actively shares his or her faith in the process of discipling others. A discipler carries out the Great Commission from Matthew 28:18-20.
- *Coach*—a discipler who trains and assists new disciplers as they disciple others
- *Coaching cluster*—a small group of new disciplers using *The Adventure of Discipling Others* with or without a coach
- *Discipleship group*—a small group of growing disciples
- *Disciplemaking*—the whole process or full spectrum of reaching the lost with the gospel, discipling people in their intimacy and walk with Christ, and equipping spiritual laborers and leaders
- *Life-to-life*—the dynamic of sharing the reality of Christ and the truth of Scripture through a personal relationship
- *Intentional*—done with purpose; a resolve to participate in discipleship and disciplemaking
- *Spiritual multiplication*—developing spiritual generations as modeled in 2 Timothy 2:2

In the generational concept found in 2 Timothy 2:2, each role represents the following:

- The coach represents the first generation (Paul)
- The new discipler represents the second generation (Timothy)
- The growing disciple represents the third generation (faithful men and women)

ASSUMPTIONS

The Adventure of Discipling Others includes some basic assumptions. We realize that some of these may not fit your situation, and you'll have to adjust your expectations as you implement this material.

The new discipler has a solid, personal walk with Christ. He or she has experienced the reality of what is to be passed on to others. The new discipler has firsthand experience with the tools and materials that he or she will use to help others. While this person may not feel adequate or competent, he or she is comfortable modeling a walk with Christ.

During the sessions in this book, we encourage the new discipler to maintain three discipleship life skills: devotional time, Scripture memory, and outreach. We assume that each new discipler has the knowledge to carry out these activities, yet he or she needs encouragement and accountability.

New disciplers are eager to minister in the lives of others. They have a heart for people and a desire to see others mature. During the process of using *The Adventure of Discipling Others,* this heart and vision will grow and become grounded more in Scripture.

Disciplemaking is best learned in the context of actual ministry. Discipling others isn't a classroom skill. Disciplers must combine knowledge with actual experiences of ministering to others. Each new discipler should have at least one person to disciple during the learning period.

Some leaders are willing to function as mentor-coaches for new disciplers. These coaches must be influencers who have the heart, vision, and skills of a discipler. But as coaches, they assume the role of grandparents rather than parents as they help the new disciplers.

New disciplers need to be willing to commit at least one year to an on-the-job learning process. This means they have or find the freedom in their schedule and responsibilities to give their time and attention to investing in at least one person.

CORE COMPONENTS

We've tried to weave four strands of concentration throughout *The Adventure of Discipling Others*.

1. DISCIPLEMAKING VISION

The first strand has to do with developing a solid biblical vision for disciplemaking. Vision is like the seed of the future tree. *The Adventure of Discipling Others* will help ground new disciplers in a lifelong conviction for discipling others. Regardless of their gifting and responsibilities, they'll develop a heart and vision for discipling others that will permeate their understanding of God's call on their lives. They'll come to understand that the heart of the Great Commission is disciplemaking, and that the key to disciplemaking is a committed discipler.

2. MINISTERING LIFE-TO-LIFE

The second interwoven strand is life-to-life ministry. A life-to-life ministry is more than passing on knowledge. It's more than meeting as a small group or one to one. A life-to-life discipler shares the reality of Christ and the truth of Scripture through a personal relationship that includes authenticity and transparency.

Few people will have a platform ministry of teaching or preaching. Others will lead small groups. But everyone can have a life-to-life ministry. *The Adventure of Discipling Others* develops the understanding and skills people need for this critical ministry dynamic.

3. SPIRITUAL POWER

The third strand is reliance on God's resources. Transformation occurs as we complement what God is doing in the lives of those we minister to. Staying in step with God and His Spirit is an essential part of disciplemaking ministry. Without reliance on God, our own endeavors are useless. Spiritual power comes as we grasp the resources of God—faith, prayer, His promises, the Holy Spirit—and are willing to see the reality of the spiritual warfare we're engaged in.

4. LEARNING ENVIRONMENT

The final strand is creating a learning atmosphere in the context of community and the mutual support of others. Maintaining core discipleship skills enables disciplers to abide in Christ and model discipleship. Having others to share with and challenge us keeps the cutting edge sharp. An environment of accountability provides encouragement, and support helps each of us strive for excellence. That's why we will be referring you to your cluster group frequently.

Disciplers model and experience these four strands as they become equipped to disciple others. These same four are also key to the discipler's own ministry. The discipler will modify the content but needs to create the same environment with growing disciples.

Finally, these important strands are *not* treated independently in *The Adventure of Discipling Others*. We've tried to integrate them and weave them throughout the material. They're not stand-alone topics, but are meant to be an environment that needs to be continually cultivated and experienced.

WHO'LL BENEFIT FROM *THE ADVENTURE OF DISCIPLING OTHERS*?

AUDIENCE 1

Maturing disciples who are established in the basics of the Christian life and now desire to help others become established as disciples. They desire to become intentional about reproducing their life of faith in the lives of others. They desire to see new Christians follow Christ and personalize the Great Commandment and Great Commission.

AUDIENCE 2

Disciplemaking leaders who want to develop and coach new disciplers. Coaches may be leaders of small groups or a small-group ministry, or are helping maturing disciples. They could be pastors or lay leaders who are developing multiplying ministries. This material will help them understand discipling at a deeper level so they can successfully train new disciplers.

AUDIENCE 3

Small-group leaders who've taken their group through a discipling course like The Navigators' 2:7 Series can use The Adventure of Discipling Others as the next phase of training. The leaders now become coaches who enable the new disciples to begin their own discipling ministries. These new disciplers have already experienced the disciplemaking process and are familiar with the basic tools for discipling others.

AUDIENCE 4

Small-group leaders who want to add a more focused discipling component to their existing small group. These leaders have already established a small-group community, which may include some Bible study. They'll be able to complement their existing ministries with intentional, individual discipling as they lead the small group.

Many small-group leaders develop on the job by leading a small group with (or without) training in small-group dynamics. Few receive mentoring in how to intentionally develop disciples within the group. *The Adventure of Discipling Others* focuses on developing disciples one at a time through the context of life-to-life. The small group is a supplement to the disciplemaking process. Using *The Adventure of Discipling Others* doesn't require a person to lead a small group. However, it will help people who are small-group leaders to focus on individual development as they lead their groups.

AUDIENCE 5

Leaders of small-group ministries. The Adventure of Discipling Others is ideal for use in the context of a small-group leaders' training program. After being taught basic small-group dynamics, group leaders can learn how to become more intentional in bringing about maturity in the lives of those within their small groups. A monthly training format can assist the ongoing development of a church's small-group leaders.

USING *THE ADVENTURE OF DISCIPLING OTHERS*

This material is arranged to allow for flexibility in the training and development of new disciplers. The structure of twelve sessions forms the heart of the training process.

As coaches become more familiar with the material, they may make adjustments that will more adequately meet the needs of their new disciplers. The recommended twelve-session plan is a starting point; it's not intended to be rigid. Coaches can modify it to meet their needs and the needs of those involved with them.

The core program recognizes that each discipler has a limited amount of time to invest in ministry. Life for the average person in our culture is extremely busy and complex. Carving out time to invest in others in addition to receiving training requires a delicate balance.

We suggest that groups complete the first four training sessions *weekly,* then do the following eight sessions *monthly.* This makes Module 1 important.

During the final eight sessions, disciplers can meet weekly with their potential disciples. In addition, they'll meet monthly with their cluster group of new disciplers. This total structure involves a nine-month ministry period that easily fits into a calendar or school year.

USING *THE ADVENTURE OF DISCIPLING OTHERS* IN SMALL GROUPS

Each training session uses a combination of tools, including a Bible study that group members need to prepare in advance, article(s), and "Tips for Discipling," all of which disciplers need to read before the subsequent training session. In addition to the Bible studies and articles, each discipler should maintain three basic spiritual disciplines:

- A personal daily devotional life
- Scripture memory
- A witness among the lost

The format of each training session provides both the structure for sharing these disciplines and the personal accountability to keep maintaining them.

EXPECTATIONS

1. New disciplers must:

- Attend the two- to three-hour training sessions
- Fully prepare homework assignments

- Meet regularly with at least one growing disciple
- Maintain their own personal walk with Christ

2. During each learning session, the group will:

- Discuss the assigned material
- Discuss ministry progress and development
- Share from their personal walks as disciples around three core disciplines:

  Devotional life
  Scripture memory
  Outreach

- Pray together

3. In addition to maintaining their personal walks with Christ, the group members are required to spend two hours in preparation. While some may spend more time, this is a general guideline.

SUGGESTED SESSION FORMAT

It will take a minimum of two-and-a-half hours for most small groups to cover the content in each session. If a group is larger, it will take more time—three hours—if each person is to have a chance to share.

Time	(Total)	Content
15	(0:15)	Interact casually and connect relationally
15	(0:30)	Share from personal devotional times and review Scripture memory
60	(1:30)	Discuss current Bible study
30	(2:00)	Discuss current article
30	(2:30)	Discuss discipling process and experiences, and pray

For we are God's fellow workers; you are God's field, God's building. By the grace
God has given me, I laid a foundation as an expert builder, and someone else is building on it. But each one should be careful how he builds.

1 CORINTHIANS 3:9-10

Suggested Scripture Memory

Session	Title	Recommended verses	Optional verses
Session 1	The Discipling Vision		
Session 2	The Great Commission	Matthew 28:18-20	
Session 3	Description of a Disciple	John 15:8	
Session 4	Ministering Life-to-Life	1 Thessalonians 2:7-8	
Session 5	Follow Me	Matthew 4:19-20	
Session 6	Parental Prayer	Philippians 1:3-4	
Session 7	Faith and the Promises of God	2 Peter 1:4	
Session 8	Habits of the Heart	1 Timothy 4:7-8	
Session 9	The Process of Disciplemaking	Colossians 1:28-29	
Session 10	The Importance of the Word	2 Timothy 3:16-17	
Session 11	The Value of Each Individual	Isaiah 60:22	
Session 12	Spiritual Generations	2 Timothy 2:2	

Discipling Syllabus

Session	Bible Study	Article	Tips for Discipling	Personal Growth	Scripture memory	Discipling process
Initial		Preface; Introduction		Get acquainted		Determine ground rules
MODULE 1: Understanding the Blueprint						
1	The Discipling Vision	Who, Me? Make Disciples?; Born to Reproduce	In Pursuit of Disciples	Share devotional times		Discuss apprehensions
2	The Great Commission	Mentoring Toward Maturity	Mentoring New Disciplers	Share devotional times	Matthew 28:18-20	Develop potential list of disciples
3	Description of a Disciple	Principles of Selection	Finding the Right Person to Disciple	Share devotional times	John 15:8	Identify potential disciples
4	Ministering Life-to-Life	Mentoring Others	Guidelines and Checklist for the Discipler	Share devotional times	1 Thessalonians 2:7-8	Identify discipling materials; recruit
MODULE 2: Laying the Foundation						
5	Follow Me	Questions I'd Ask Before Following Jesus	Doing a Life-to-Life Session	Share devotional times	Matthew 4:19-20	Begin meeting with growing disciple(s)
6	Parental Prayer	The Prayers of a Leader	Link Discipling and Outreach	Share devotional times	Philippians 1:3-4	Pray for each growing disciple; discuss progress
7	Faith and the Promises of God	Living by Promises	Promises to Claim for a Disciple	Share devotional times	2 Peter 1:4	Share lessons being learned
8	Habits of the Heart	The Spiritual Disciplines	Habits Make the Difference	Share devotional times	1 Timothy 4:7-8	Share growing disciple's relationship with Christ
MODULE 3: Building the House						
9	The Process of Disciplemaking	We're in This Together	Ways to Help an Apathetic Disciple	Share devotional times	Colossians 1:28-29	Share growing disciple's appetite for Scriptures
10	The Importance of the Word	Speaking God's Language	How to Pray for Your Disciple …	Share devotional times	2 Timothy 3:16-17	Share growing disciple's evident marks of discipleship
11	The Value of Each Individual	The Importance of Every Individual	Don't Give Up Yet	Share devotional times	Isaiah 60:22	Share obstacles yet to be faced
12	Spiritual Generations	Motivation: For a Lifetime of Disciplemaking	Discipling over the Long Haul	Share devotional times	2 Timothy 2:1-2	Share progress seen and lessons learned

GETTING STARTED

- Get acquainted with the other members of your group. Locate the "Discipling Others Coaching Cluster" sheet on the next page. Ask members to fill out their sheets as other members share. Talk briefly about your personal backgrounds. Select one or two topics for each person to share, such as where they've lived, what jobs they've held, their children, interests, or hobbies.
- *IMPORTANT:* Silently read the Preface and the Introduction, and discuss briefly.
- Discuss the frequency of your cluster meetings. (For additional help in alternative scheduling, see the Leader's Guide on the CDM website.)
- Solidify the logistics for your group (meeting time, meeting length, meeting frequency, handling missed sessions, childcare).
- Highlight the ground rules for this course. Ground rules clarify what the group expects from each person. *IMPORTANT:* It's critical that every person in the group has a chance to buy into the rules the group will function by. The most important ones are listed under "Rules for the Journey" on pages 20-21, but your group needs to deliberate it's own so that each group member takes ownership.
- If there's time, ask group members to share why they're participating in this group and what some of their expectations, concerns, and anxieties might be.

DISCIPLING OTHERS COACHING CLUSTER

KEY ISSUES

- Who are we?
- What potential people are we going to pursue to build life-to-life discipling relationships?
- What kind of "covenant" rules do we all need to embrace to be successful in this new journey?

CLUSTER MEMBERS

Name: _____   Name: _____
Phone: _____   Phone: _____
E-mail: _____   E-mail: _____

Name: _____   Name: _____
Phone: _____   Phone: _____
E-mail: _____   E-mail: _____

Name: _____   Name: _____
Phone: _____   Phone: _____
E-mail: _____   E-mail: _____

Name: _____   Name: _____
Phone: _____   Phone: _____
E-mail: _____   E-mail: _____

CLUSTER LOGISTICS

Meeting time: _____
Meeting place: _____
Meeting dates: _____

RULES FOR THE JOURNEY

Discuss the ideas in the chart on the next page as commitments for your group. Feel free to change or modify anything to fit your particular group's needs. Discuss any questions you may have, especially those in the following chart. Make sure you take time to add or modify any the group finds helpful.

ASSIGNMENT FOR SESSION 1: THE DISCIPLING VISION

- Reread and make notes on the Introduction.
- Read the article "Who, Me? Make Disciples?"
- Read the article "Born to Reproduce."
- Read Tips for Discipling: "In Pursuit of Disciples."

Guideline	Changes or improvements
Make a commitment to the group, making attendance a priority.	
Give support and encouragement to the other members of the group.	
Faithfully carry out the assignments for the course.	
Seek to become a discipler of others by the grace and Spirit of God.	
Share both the joys and the struggles of your faith journey in discipling others.	
Hold in confidence all that is shared in the group. Others:	

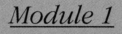

Module 1

UNDERSTANDING THE BLUEPRINT

THE DISCIPLING VISION

LESSON PLAN

- Review the Introduction.
- Ask, "How well are we doing in our churches at spiritual reproducing?"
- Discuss "Who, Me? Make Disciples?" by Lee Brase. If you didn't assign this prior to this session, give time for group members to read the article and highlight key ideas before you discuss it as a group. Utilize questions at the end of the article as appropriate.
- Discuss "Born to Reproduce" by Dawson Trotman. Again, if necessary, give time for members to read the article and highlight key ideas before you discuss it as a group. Utilize questions at the end of the article as appropriate.
- Be sure to discuss the practical side of disciplemaking in the Tips for Discipling: "In Pursuit of Disciples."
- Launch the sharing of individual devotional times by talking about one of your recent experiences regarding a time with God.
- Discuss any apprehensions people may have as they begin this course.

ASSIGNMENT FOR SESSION 2: THE GREAT COMMISSION

- Prepare the Bible study "The Great Commission."
- Read the article "Mentoring Toward Maturity."
- Write out and memorize Matthew 28:18-20 or optional verse(s).
- Continue your personal devotional times using highlights or a journal.
- Read the Tips for Discipling: "Mentoring New Disciplers."

GROUP PRAYER REQUESTS

Who, Me? Make Disciples?

by Lee Brase

THE KEY IS NOT in the technique but in the heart.

Who has had a great influence on your life for Christ? What qualities did this person have that enabled him to have such an influence on you?

I've asked hundreds of people these questions. No one has ever said he was helped because the person was so intellectual, had such a dynamic personality, or was so good-looking! Neither do people mention the syllabus they studied, or the hoops they jumped through.

What they do say is that it was the person's relationship with people and God that really mattered. "He really cared for me." "She had such a genuine interest in me." "He believed in me." "He had a close walk with God." "She took the time to listen to me." "She was open and honest."

When the disciples heard Jesus say, "Go and make disciples" (Matthew 28:19), they responded, "Yes, Lord," and did it. Today, when we hear this same command, we respond, "Who, me? I'm not eloquent. I haven't been trained. No one's ever shown me how to do this." However, the qualities of a disciplemaker are available to all of us. To emphasize this truth, our Lord seemed deliberately to train those who were "unschooled, ordinary men" (Acts 4:13) and leave His work in their hands.

I've discovered three essential qualities of a disciplemaker. God expects them of any Christian. If you have them, you can expect God to use you to help others grow.

1. A WALK OF FAITH

When God appeared to Moses through the burning bush, He told him He had seen Israel's misery and wanted Moses to go back and lead them out of Egypt. Moses' immediate response was to question God's judgment in selecting him (Exodus 3:11). Forty years earlier, Moses had attempted to help the Israelites and failed miserably. He'd run from Egypt with an Israelite's question ringing in his mind: "Who made you ruler and judge over us?" (Exodus 2:14).

Most of us, like Moses, have attempted to help people along the way and failed. The second person I tried to disciple dropped me a note after several months of meeting regularly: "I want nothing more to do with you or God." I wanted to do what Moses did—run to the desert and work with sheep. It was hard to get excited about discipling the next person who needed my help.

Where do we find the courage to get involved in people's lives after we've failed? Or what about the courage to help that very first person?

The answer lies in God's response to Moses. He gave the promise, "I will be with you" (Exodus 3:12).

God didn't try to encourage Moses to rely on his ability and training. He simply assured Moses of His presence. Jesus made the same promise when He commissioned the apostles to go and make disciples. None of these men had a good record of accomplishment. Yet, each risked his life to disciple people all over the world. Jesus backed up their commission to make disciples with two statements: "All authority in heaven and on earth has been given to me" and "Surely I am with you always, to the very end of the age" (Matthew 28:18; Matthew 28:20).

If Jesus Christ were here in human form and went with us to help someone, we'd go with great confidence that the person would receive what he needed. That's exactly what He's promised to do. Faith is the ability to believe that what God says is more real than what our eyes see. We can rely on the promise of His presence.

People who trust God make excellent disciplemakers. Knowing that only God can change lives, they become people of prayer. They see God work way beyond their natural abilities. God receives the glory only when our ministries go beyond what we could do on our own.

Believing God also frees us to believe in people. I remember a time when my spiritual growth accelerated. Why? The person helping me believed in God and believed in me. He believed God could do things with my life I never dreamed possible. I grew in accordance with his faith.

It was only natural that I should then believe God for the people I was discipling. Some years later, a man I'd discipled said he knew his solid walk with Christ had occurred because, "You believed in me." He boiled down our hundreds of hours together to that one statement.

"The one who calls you is faithful and he will do it" (1 Thessalonians 5:24). A discipler has faith that God will work through him to make disciples.

2. A HEART FOR PEOPLE

A disciplemaker must love those he wants to help. In addition, love sees people the way they are and then serves them.

A disciplemaker's goal is to build people up in Christ. The Apostle Paul said, "Knowledge puffs up, but love builds up" (1 Corinthians 8:1)..It was Paul's love, more than his knowledge and abilities, that established hundreds of Christians throughout Asia Minor and Europe. He was able to write to the Thessalonians, "As apostles of Christ we could have been a burden to you, but we were gentle among you, like a mother caring for her little children. We loved you so much that we were delighted to share with you not only the gospel of God but our lives as well, because you had become so dear to us" (1 Thessalonians 2:6-8).

Love, like faith, expresses itself in action. That's why Paul went on to say to the Thessalonians, "Surely you remember, brothers, our toil and hardship; we worked night and day in order not to be a burden to anyone while we preached the gospel of God to you" (1 Thessalonians 2:9). Paul called himself a servant to the Corinthians (1 Corinthians 4:1). Serving is love in action.

Several years ago, a Chinese Christian stayed with us for a month. He observed how I tried to train people using my programs. My experience and knowledge limited the training. Finally, he confronted me: "You train a man and he can only become what you are, but if you serve a man, the sky is the limit."

This liberated me from thinking of discipling as getting people through programs and methods. I began thinking of how to serve each person to help him become more mature in Christ. The person, not my program, became the focus. Those who want to co-labor with Christ in others' lives are not to "lord it over them" (Matthew 20:25), but to serve them.

Every human being has needs and burdens. They're necessary for growth. We help people grow when we "carry each other's burdens" (Galatians 6:2). Doing this takes a servant's heart.

We have a beautiful picture of serving in Jesus' life. "Come to me, all you who are weary and burdened, and I will give you rest" (Matthew 11:28). His invitation came at the end of a very difficult day. Jesus had just had to denounce the cities in which most of His miracles had been performed because the people didn't repent (Matthew 11:20). People who questioned His motives had called Him "a glutton and a drunkard" (Matthew 11:19). And John the Baptist had just sent some of his disciples to ask Jesus, "Are you the one who was to come, or should we expect someone else?" (Matthew 11:2).

Jesus had had enough disappointments that day to make most of us withdraw, sulk, and cry. However, He invited others to bring their cares and burdens to Him.

Love gives us the capacity to serve others even when our burdens are heavy. It enables us to put our cares aside for the moment and give ourselves to someone else. Without love, we'll never truly disciple others. They'll have to fit into our schedule and needs—and they won't, and shouldn't have to.

3. A LIFE PATTERNED AFTER JESUS

A disciple follows Jesus Christ with the intent of becoming like Him. This implies two things: That he focuses on Christ and that he's a learner.

A FOCUS ON JESUS

Imagine what would have happened if Jesus had called to Peter and Andrew, "Leave your boat and nets and come join my Bible study class" and three years later had said, "Go into all the world and promote my three-year discipleship program." No one would give their lives for a class or a program. These things aren't worthy of our lives. But Jesus Christ is. Everything in life finds meaning when we properly relate to Him. He leads, we follow. We know we're disciples when we allow Jesus Christ to order our lives—family, finances, career, pleasures, friendships, possessions, etc.

J. I. Packer was once asked what he saw as the greatest need in the Church in the Western world. His response was that we must get back to the centrality of Jesus Christ. Paul said to the Corinthians, "But I am afraid that . . . your minds may somehow be led astray from your sincere and pure devotion to Christ" (2 Corinthians 11:3). One of the major reasons many Christians avoid discipling others is that they have lost that pure devotion to Christ. They give themselves to activities, classes, and programs, and that's all they have to offer others.

One of the best disciplemakers I know was raised as a flower farmer. Because of the needs on the farm, Dirk had to drop out of high school. However, his mind was alert and his heart set on Christ. This drove him to the Bible. He memorized a verse every day and then meditated on it while working. Such a heart for the Lord was contagious. Before long, university students sought him out for help in their lives. It was the Person of Christ in his life that attracted others.

A TEACHABLE SPIRIT

The disciplemaker is a learner. He is open to change. For him, the entire world is a classroom. He not only teaches the one he's discipling, but also learns from him. The wisest man on earth said, "Better a poor but wise youth than an old but foolish king who no longer knows how to take warning" (Ecclesiastes 4:13).

The disciplemaker studies people and seeks to become skillful in helping them. Paul said he discipled the Corinthians "as an expert builder" (1 Corinthians 3:10). He became that by observing them so well that he knew just what they needed.

Bob and Dave have a ministry together that reaches into several states. They are both well-educated, mature men. They know enough about the Lord, His Word, and ministry techniques to put most of us to shame. Yet, as I have traveled with them, I have seen them constantly put themselves in the position of learners rather than the ones with the answers. As a result, they always have people around them asking questions.

YES, YOU!

Three facts stand out for us as Christ's people:

1. The Lord wants us to make disciples. He commissioned us to do it when He said, "Go and make disciples of all nations" (Matthew 28:19).

2. Plenty of people need to be discipled. "The harvest is plentiful but the workers are few" (Matthew 9:37).

3. Any of us can disciple others if we believe God, love people, and follow Christ with the intent of becoming like Him.

Don't wait until you feel capable. The heart of the disciplemaker is his character, not his skills. Step out in faith, invest your life in someone else, and pick up the skills as you go along.[1]

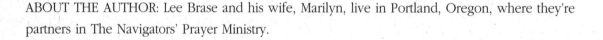

ABOUT THE AUTHOR: Lee Brase and his wife, Marilyn, live in Portland, Oregon, where they're partners in The Navigators' Prayer Ministry.

QUESTIONS FOR REFLECTION

1. Who has had a great influence on you? What were some of the qualities of people who you found inspiring as you were formulating your spiritual path?

2. Who is someone you tried to influence but failed? As you now look back, why did you fail?

3. One Brazilian disciplemaker was asked what he felt was the key to the success of many generations of disciples in his country. After thinking on it for a few days he replied, "John 13:34-35." Why do you think he thought this was the key?

Born to Reproduce

by Dawson E. Trotman

IN APRIL 1933, LES SPENCER *was a young sailor aboard the U.S.S. West Virginia off the California coast. While washing dishes, he received a telegram: "Meet me at the San Pedro dock at 4 p.m. I will be wearing a dark coat, light trousers and tan shoes. Dawson Trotman."*

Les was troubled and suspicious. He didn't know Dawson Trotman. But curiosity got the best of him, and he arrived at the dock just before 4 p.m. Suddenly a man emerged from the crowd of Navy men. He stuck out his hand and made fast friends with the sailor.

For the next three months, Dawson spent hours teaching Les about the Bible, evangelism, and follow-up. Then Les brought his friend Gurney Harris to the Trotman house. He told Daws, "Give this man what you have been giving me."

Dawson looked at Les and replied, "No, I'm not going to. You're going to give this man what I've been giving to you."

Les protested, "But I've never been to Bible school, and besides I don't know how to do it. I can't."

Daws replied, "If you can't give to Gurney what I've given to you, then I've failed."

Les accepted the challenge. And Daws, founder of The Navigators, began the principle of spiritual multiplication. He believed Christians should not just make disciples, they should reproduce disciples who are also disciplemakers. Only then will laborers increase in the unplucked, spiritual harvest.

———◆———

A few years ago, while visiting Edinburgh, Scotland, I stood on High Street just down from the castle. As I stood there, I saw a father and a mother coming toward me pushing a baby carriage. They looked very happy, were well dressed, and apparently were well to do.

I watched them for a little while as they walked on and thought how beautiful it is that God permits a man to choose one woman who seems the most beautiful and lovely to him, and she chooses him out of all the men whom she has ever known. Then they separate themselves to one another, and God in His plan gives them the means of reproduction! It is a wonderful thing that a little child should be born into their family, having some of the father's characteristics and some of the mother's, some of his looks and some of hers.

Seeing that little one made me feel homesick for my own children whom I dearly love and whose faces I had not seen for some time. As I continued to stand there I saw another baby carriage coming in my direction. It was a secondhand affair and very wobbly. Obviously, the father and mother were poor. Both were dressed poorly and plainly, but when I indicated my interest in seeing their baby, they stopped and with the same pride as the other parents let me view their little, pink-cheeked, beautiful-eyed child.

I thought as these went on their way, "God gave this little baby whose parents are poor everything that He gave the other. It has five little fingers on each hand, a little mouth, and two eyes. Properly cared for, those little hands may someday be the hands of an artist or a musician."

Then this other thought came to me, "Isn't it wonderful that God did not select the wealthy and the educated and say, 'You can have children,' and to the poor and the uneducated say, 'You cannot.' Everyone on earth has that privilege."

The first order ever given to man was that he "be fruitful and multiply." In other words, he was to reproduce after his own kind. God did not tell Adam and Eve, our first parents, to be spiritual. They were already in His image. Sin had not yet come in. He just said, "Multiply. I want more just like you, more in My own image."

Of course, the image was marred. But Adam and Eve had children. They began to multiply. There came a time, however, when God had to destroy most of the flesh that had been born. He started over with eight people. The more than two billion people who are on earth today came from the eight who were in the ark because they were fruitful and multiplied.

HINDRANCES

Only a few things will ever keep human beings from multiplying themselves in the physical realm. One is that they never marry. If they are not united, they will not reproduce. This is a truth, which Christians need to grasp with reference to spiritual reproduction. When a person becomes a child of God, he should realize that he is to live in union with Jesus Christ if he is going to win others to the Savior.

Another factor that can hinder reproduction is disease or impairment to some part of the body that is needed for reproductive purposes. In the spiritual realm sin is the disease that can keep one from winning the lost.

One other thing that can keep people from having children is immaturity. God in His wisdom saw to it that little children cannot have babies. A little boy must first grow to sufficient maturity to be able to earn a living, and a little girl must be old enough to care for a baby.

Everyone should be born again. That is God's desire. God never intended that man should merely live and die—be a walking corpse to be laid in the ground. The vast majority of people know that there is something beyond the grave, and so each one who is born into God's family should seek others to be born again.

A person is born again when he receives Jesus Christ. "But as many as received Him, to them gave He power to become the sons of God . . . Which were born, not of blood, not of the will of the flesh, nor of the will of man, but of God" (John 1:12-13). This is the new birth. It is God's plan that these new babes in Christ grow. All provision is made for their growth into maturity, and then they are to multiply—not only the rich or the educated, but all alike. Every person who is born into God's family is to multiply.

In the physical realm when your children have children, you become a grandparent. Your parents are then great-grandparents, and theirs are great-great-grandparents. And so it should be in the spiritual.

SPIRITUAL BABES

Whenever you find a Christian who is not leading men and women to Christ, something is wrong. He may still be a babe. I do not mean that he does not know a lot of doctrine and is not well informed through hearing good preaching. I know many people who can argue the pre-, the post- and the amillennial position and who know much about dispensations, but who are still immature. Paul said of some such in Corinth, "And I, brethren, could not speak unto you as unto spiritual (or mature), but as unto carnal, even as unto babes . . . " (1 Corinthians 3:1).

Because they were babes, they were immature, incapable of spiritual reproduction. In other words, they could not help other people to be born again.

Paul continued, "I have fed you with milk, and not with meat: for hitherto ye were not able to bear it . . . ye are yet carnal (or babes): for . . . there is among you envying, and strife, and divisions . . . " (1 Corinthians 3:2-3). I know a lot of church members, Sunday school teachers and members of the women's missionary society who will say to each other, "Have you heard about so and so?" and pass along some gossip. Such have done an abominable thing in the sight of God. How horrible it is when a Christian hears something and spreads the story! The Book says, "These six things doth the Lord hate; yea, seven are an abomination unto Him . . . a lying tongue . . . " (Proverbs 6:16-17). Oh, the Christians I know, both men and women, who let lying come in! "He that soweth discord among brethren" (Proverbs 6:19) is another.

This is walking as a babe, and I believe that it is one of the basic reasons why some Christians do not have people born again into God's family through them. They are sick spiritually. There is something wrong. There is a spiritual disease in their lives. They are immature. There is not that union with Christ.

But when all things are right between you and the Lord, regardless of how much or how little you may know intellectually from the standpoint of the world, you can be a spiritual parent. And that, incidentally, may even be when you are very young in the Lord.

A young woman works at the telephone desk in our office in Colorado Springs. A year and a half ago she was associated with the young Communist league in Great Britain. She heard Billy Graham and accepted the Lord Jesus Christ. Soon she and a couple other girls in her art and drama school were used of the Lord to win some girls to Christ. We taught Pat and some of the others, and they in turn taught the girls whom they led to Christ. Some of these too are training their friends. Patricia is a great-grandmother already, though she is only about a year and four months old in the Lord.

Some time ago I talked to twenty-nine missionary candidates. They were graduates of universities or Bible schools or seminaries. As a member of the board I interviewed each one over a period of five days, giving each candidate from half an hour to an hour. Among the questions I asked were two, which are very important. The first one had to do with their devotional life, "How is the time you spend with the Lord? Do you feel that your devotional life is what the Lord would have it to be?"

Out of this particular group of twenty-nine, only one person said, "I believe my devotional life is what it ought to be." To the others my question then was, "Why is your devotional life not what it should be?"

"Well, you see, I am here at this summer institute," was a common reply. "We have a concentrated course. We do a year's work in only ten weeks. We are so busy."

I said, "All right. Let's back up to when you were in college. Did you have victory in your devotional life then?"

"Well, not exactly."

We traced back and found that never since they came to know the Savior had they had a period of victory in their devotional lives. That was one of the reasons for their sterility—lack of communion with Christ.

The other question I asked them was, "You are going out to the foreign field. You hope to be used by the Lord in winning men and women to Christ. Is that right?"

"Yes."

"You want them to go on and live the victorious life, don't you? You don't want them just to make a decision and then go back into the world, do you?"

"No."

"Then may I ask you something more? How many persons do you know by name today who were won to Christ by you and are living for Him?"

The majority had to admit that they were ready to cross an ocean and learn a foreign language, but they had not won their first soul who was going on with Jesus Christ. A number of them said that they got many people to go to church; others said they had persuaded some to go forward when the invitation was given.

I asked, "Are they living for Christ now?" Their eyes dropped. I then continued, "How do you expect that by crossing an ocean and speaking in a foreign language with people who are suspicious of you, whose way of life is unfamiliar, you will be able to do there what you have not yet done here?"

These questions do not apply to missionaries and prospective missionaries only. They apply to all of God's people. Every one of His children ought to be a reproducer.

Are you producing? If not, why not? Is it because of a lack of communion with Christ, your Lord, that closeness of fellowship, which is part of the great plan? Or is it some sin in your life, an unconfessed something, that has stopped the flow? Or is it that you are still a babe? "For when for the time ye ought to be teachers, ye have need that one teach you again . . . " (Hebrews 5:12).

HOW TO PRODUCE REPRODUCERS

The reason that we are not getting this Gospel to the ends of the earth is not because it is not potent enough.

Twenty-three years ago we took a born-again sailor and spent some time with him, showing him how to reproduce spiritually after his kind. It took time, lots of time. It was not a hurried, thirty-minute challenge in a church service and a hasty good-bye with an invitation to come back next week. We spent time together. We took care of his problems and taught him not only to hear God's Word and to read it, but also how to study it. We taught him how to fill the quiver of his heart with the arrows of God's Word, so that the Spirit of God could lift an arrow from his heart and place it to the bow of his lips and pierce a heart for Christ.

He found a number of men on his ship, but none of them would go all out for the Lord. They would go to church, but when it came right down to doing something, they were "also rans." He came to me after a month of this and said, "Dawson, I can't get any of these guys on the ship to get down to business."

I said to him, "Listen, ask God to give you one. You can't have two until you have one. Ask God to give you a man after your own heart."

He began to pray. One day he came to me and said, "I think I've found him." Later he brought the young fellow over. Three months from the time that I started to work with him, he had found a man of like heart. This first sailor was not the kind of man you had to push and give prizes to before he would do something. He loved the Lord and was willing to pay a price to produce. He worked with this new babe in Christ, and those two fellows began to grow and spiritually reproduce. On that ship 125 men found the Savior before it was sunk at Pearl Harbor. Men off that first battleship are in four continents of the world as missionaries today. It was necessary to make a start, however. The devil's trick is to stop anything like this if he can before it gets started. He will stop you, too, if you let him.

I believe that is why Satan puts all his efforts into getting the Christian busy, busy, but not producing. Men, where is your man? Women, where is your woman? Where is the one whom you led to Christ and who is now going on with Him?

The curse of today is that we are too busy. I am not talking about being busy earning money to buy food. I am talking about being busy doing Christian things. We have spiritual activities with little productivity. And productivity comes as a result of what we call "follow-up."

BEGINNING OF FOLLOW-UP

One day, years ago, I was driving along in my little Model T Ford and saw a young man walking down the street. I stopped and picked him up. As he got into the car, he swore and said, "It's sure tough to get a ride." I never hear a man take my Savior's name in vain but what my heart aches. I reached into my pocket for a tract and said, "Lad, read this."

He looked up at me and said, "Haven't I seen you somewhere before?"

I looked at him closely. He looked like someone I should know. We figured out that we had met the year before on the same road. He was on his way to a golf course to caddy when I picked him up. He had gotten into my car and had started out the same way with the name "Jesus Christ." I had taken exception to his use of that name and had opened up the New Testament and shown him the way of salvation. He had accepted Jesus Christ as his Savior. In parting I had given him Philippians 1:6: "Being confident of this very thing, that He which hath begun a good work in you will perform it until the day of Jesus Christ." "God bless you, son. Read this," I said, and sped on my merry way.

A year later, there was no more evidence of the new birth and the new creature in this young man than if he had never heard of Jesus Christ.

I had a great passion to win souls and that was my great passion. But after I met this boy the second time on the way to the golf course, I began to go back and find some of my "converts." I want to tell you, I was sick at heart. It seemed that Philippians 1:6 was not working.

Paul said to the elders of the church at Ephesus, "Take heed . . . to all the flock, over which the Holy Spirit has made you overseers" (Acts 20:28). You cannot make God the overseer. He makes you the overseer.

Before, I had forgotten to follow up the people God had reached through me. But from then on I began to spend time helping them. That is why sometime later when that first sailor came to me; I saw the value of spending three months with him. I saw an Isaac in him. Isaac had Jacob, and Jacob had the twelve, and all the rest of the nation came through them.

IT TAKES TIME TO DO GOD'S WORK

You can lead a soul to Christ from twenty minutes to a couple of hours. But it takes from twenty weeks to a couple of years to get him on the road to maturity, victorious over the sins and the recurring problems that come along. He must learn how to make right decisions. He must be warned of the various "isms" that are likely to reach out with their octopus arms and pull him in and sidetrack him.

But when you get yourself someone, you have doubled your ministry—in fact, you have more than doubled your ministry. Do you know why? When you teach him, he sees how it is done and he imitates you.

If I were the minister of a church and had deacons or elders to pass the plate and choir members to sing, I would say, "Thank God for your help. We need you. Praise the Lord for these extra things that you do," but I would keep pressing home the big job: "Be fruitful and multiply." All these other things are incidental to the supreme tasks of winning a man or woman to Jesus Christ and then helping him or her to go on.

Where is your man? Where is your woman? Do you have one? You can ask God for one. Search your hearts. Ask the Lord, "Am I spiritually sterile? If I am, why am I?" Soulwinners are not soulwinners because of what they know, but because of the Person they know, how well they know Him and how much they long for others to know Him.

Effects obey their causes by irresistible laws. When you sow the seed of God's Word you will get results. Not every heart will receive the Word but some will and the new birth will take place. When a soul is born, give it the care that Paul gave new believers. Paul believed in follow-up work. He was a busy evangelist, but he took time for follow-up. The New Testament is largely made up of the letters of Paul, which were follow-up letters to the converts.

The Gospel spread to the known world during the first century without radio, television, or the printing press because of these produced men who were reproducing. But today we have a lot of pew-sitters—people think that if they are faithful in church attendance, put good-sized gifts into the offering plate, and get people to come, they have done their part.

Where is your man? Where is your woman? Where is your boy? Where is your girl?

Load your heart with this precious Seed. You will find that God will direct you to those whom you can lead to Christ. There are many hearts ready for the Gospel now.[2]

QUESTIONS FOR REFLECTION

1. Dawson said in the article, "Whenever you find a Christian who is not leading men and women to Christ, something is wrong" and "Are you producing? If not, why not?" How do you respond to these statements?

2. Dawson makes the statement, "The curse of today is that we are too busy . . . doing Christian things . . . spiritual activities with little productivity." Evaluate your time by comparing your spiritual activities with spiritual productivity.

► TIPS FOR DISCIPLING

In Pursuit of Disciples
by Daryl Donovan

Jesus was always pursuing people for the kingdom of God. Have you developed a "sit and wait" instead of a "go and make" attitude about disciplemaking?

GET MOVING

PRAY
Ask God to show you those He wants you to pursue. Jesus chose the twelve after a full night of prayer.

LOOK
Watch for people with a desire to grow.

ASK
Don't wait for potential disciples to come to you. Once God points someone out to you, approach him or her about a discipling relationship.

COMMIT
Jesus shared more than His teaching with His disciples. He shared His life.

ENCOURAGE
Come alongside the person God gives you to disciple to form a healthy relationship of Christian love and mutual accountability.[3]

THE GREAT COMMISSION

LESSON PLAN

- Have a few group members share about their spiritual journey each week until all have had the opportunity to tell their stories.
- Have a few share a recent highlight from personal devotional times.
- Review Matthew 28:18-20. (For additional help in learning how to memorize Scripture, see The Navigators' 2:7 Series or the Topical Memory System.) Seek help on the website www.navigators.org/CDM/ADO for other ideas.
- Discuss the Bible study "The Great Commission."
- Discuss the article "Mentoring Toward Maturity."
- Share the names of potential new disciples that members are praying about discipling. Begin recording names on the "Potential Disciples List" found in appendix C (page 218).
- Discuss Tips for Discipling: "Mentoring New Disciplers."

ASSIGNMENT FOR SESSION 3: DESCRIPTION OF A DISCIPLE

- Prepare the "Description of a Disciple" Bible study.
- Read the article "Principles of Selection."
- *Important:* Read the material in Discipling Resources in appendix A (page 216).
- Memorize John 15:8.
- Review past Scripture memory verses.
- Read Tips for Discipling: "Finding the Right Person to Disciple."
- Pray over potential person(s) you can begin to disciple.

GROUP PRAYER REQUESTS

▶ BIBLE STUDY

THE GREAT COMMISSION

KEY ISSUES

- What is the Great Commission from the Gospels?
- How does Matthew summarize the Great Commission?
- What is every believer's relationship to the gospel and the Great Commission?

Jesus gave His apprentices some famous last words:

> Jesus, undeterred, went right ahead and gave his charge: "God authorized and commanded me to commission you: Go out and train everyone you meet, far and near, in this way of life, marking them by baptism in the threefold name: Father, Son, and Holy Spirit. Then instruct them in the practice of all I have commanded you. I'll be with you as you do this, day after day after day, right up to the end of the age. (Matthew 28:18-20, MSG)

> The Great Commission is our beacon light in the midst of human fog and conjecture.
>
> GEORGE PETERS

> There is more in the Great Commission than a person can dream about, or think about, or do about, even if he had ten lifetimes.
>
> JOHN MCGEE

What has made the words of the Great Commission so motivating for so many of God's people for so long?

Is the mandate Jesus gave two thousand years ago contingent on us? What makes it so *great* if it means getting out of my comfort zone, talking to people I don't know, and having to give myself for others?

The term "Great Commission" isn't found in the Bible, but is historically attached to the mission Jesus gave to His disciples after His resurrection. It's the mission expressed in each of the Gospels and the book of Acts.

1. Define the word *commission* in your own words and then compare your definition with a dictionary's. What are the key ideas in this term?

READING THE GREAT COMMISSION

Each of the following passages expresses Christ's Great Commission. Observe the emphasis each writer expresses. Use the space below the questions to record your observations regarding the different expressions of the Great Commission. (Here is some background: The Gospels were written with the intention of having special appeal to different kinds of people, different audiences.[1])

2a. Matthew was written by a Jewish person, to a Jewish person, about a Jewish person. It has a spiritual umbrella of authority and kingdom. It was given to help the *religious-minded* embrace Jesus as King. In Matthew 28:16-20:
What is the command or active verbs?

What are the key ideas or what is the major emphasis?

What resources are described?

2b. Mark was the secretary to Peter and put emphasis on the proclamation of the good news. His gospel has an umbrella of active service and sacrifice. Mark was written for the *pragmatic-minded* to embrace Jesus as a servant. In Mark 16:15-20:
What is the command or active verbs?

What are the key ideas or what is the major emphasis?

What resources are described?

2c. Luke was a doctor who wrote of the continuity of God's plan. His gospel has an umbrella of human compassion and warmth. It was written for Gentiles, or the *unchurched-minded,* to understand that all are included in God's plan. In Luke 24:44-49:

What is the command or active verbs?

What are the key ideas or what is the major emphasis?

What resources are described?

2d. John, "the disciple whom Jesus loved," wrote of the universality of salvation. His book has an umbrella of the deity of God's Son. It was written topically and *universally* to all that they must believe in the Son of God. In John 20:19-23; 21:5-6,15-19:

What is the command or active verbs?

What are the key ideas or what is the major emphasis?

What resources are described?

2e. What ideas are common to more than one passage?

2f. What specific instructions do these passages give regarding communicating the gospel?

STUDYING THE GREAT COMMISSION

There is only one imperative verb in the Great Commission passage of Matthew 28:17-20. It is "make" disciples. All the others are clauses that support the main command. Take a closer look at Matthew 28:17-20 by answering the following questions. (You may need a dictionary or a Bible dictionary to help you study.)

3a. What does the passage state and imply regarding Jesus' authority?

3b. What does "go" or "as you are going" mean?

3c. What does the term "make disciples" imply?

3d. What's the meaning of "teaching them to observe [obey] all I have commanded you" in verse 20?

3e. Describe the concept of spiritual reproduction or spiritual generations as you find it in this passage.

OPTIONAL, FOR FURTHER THOUGHT:

• What is the significance of baptism in the discipline of others?
• Are there other questions you have that remain unanswered?

SUMMARIZING THE GREAT COMMISSION

4a. Using the four expressions of the Great Commission, write a summary statement of the Great Commission in your own words. (For example: "The Almighty God says come out of your shell and tell people about Me. Show them how to live forever. Keep the process going 'til I come again" (from an employee of American Family Insurance).

4b. Does this summary of the Great Commission apply to *you?* How?

5. God called some people in the Bible for a specific mission. Choose one of the people below and consider the common block or resistance to a commission and what God has to say about it.
   Elisha (1 Kings 19:14-20; 2 Kings 2:1-13)

   Isaiah (Isaiah 6:1-13)

   Jeremiah (Jeremiah 1:3-10,17)

   Apollos (Acts 18:24-27; 19:1; 1 Corinthians 3:4-7,22)

STEWARDSHIP AND THE GREAT COMMISSION

In Christian circles, stewardship often refers only to finances. However, a "steward" in biblical times was usually a slave or freedman who had the responsibility of managing the estate or household of someone else. The dictionary defines *steward* as someone entrusted to handle resources. The Bible uses the term metaphorically of preachers of the gospel or teachers of the Word. Scripture has a great deal to say about spiritual stewardship, especially in light of the gospel.

6a. What would you say *entrusted* means?

6b. In light of the Great Commission, what do the following verses teach about stewardship (the role or responsibility) and the steward (the person entrusted)?

Luke 12:47-48

Luke 16:10-13

1 Thessalonians 2:4

2 Timothy 1:14

2 Timothy 2:1-2

6c. Do you feel you can present an adequate expression of the gospel message to someone else? Explain your thinking.

6d. Do you view yourself as a steward of the gospel? Why, or why not?

6e. How can you begin to influence those you are discipling in their stewardship role?

SUMMARY

7. In light of the extreme busyness and complexities of living in today's world, what changes will believers have to make if they are to become serious about the Great Commission?

8. Are there any adjustments you need to make in your life where God is giving you a gentle nudge?

9. Who will you disciple?

I cannot love Christ if I cannot love every soul for which Christ died.

ST. FRANCIS OF ASSISI

Mentoring Toward Maturity

by Lynn Austin

"I DON'T KNOW WHAT to do," my neighbor Gail sobbed over the phone. "Will you please pray for me?" I grabbed my Bible and hurried next door. A fairly new Christian, Gail relied heavily on me to give advice, answer questions, and pray for her. After a year and a half, I'd supported Gail through several crises, explained many Scriptures, and prayed countless prayers for her.

"God is so good to give me a neighbor who's a mature Christian," she often said.

I enjoyed feeling needed by Gail and returned home each time satisfied that God had used me. But it bothered me that after so much time Gail hadn't grown any stronger as a Christian. This verse in Hebrews seemed to describe her: "Though by this time you ought to be teachers, you need someone to teach you the elementary truths of God's word all over again. You need milk, not solid food!" (Hebrews 5:12). Something was wrong, but I didn't know what.

As an elementary school teacher, I was studying mentoring programs where experienced teachers team up with beginners to help ease the transition into teaching. The goal of mentoring is to lead the beginner through a process of growth from dependence to independence. But in order to reach that goal, the mentoring relationship must gradually change as the mentor progresses through a series of five roles: teacher, coach, collaborator, sponsor, and counselor.

That's what's wrong, I thought. Gail's never grown in her Christian walk because my role with her has never changed. I enjoy being needed and I've kept her dependent on me, stunting her spiritual growth. Gail, who grew up in a church that relied heavily on the clergy for prayer and teaching, was content with our relationship. But I knew that God desired for Gail to "leave the elementary teachings about Christ and go on to maturity" (Hebrews 6:1).

That same year God sent Donna into my life. Our sons had met in kindergarten and quickly became best friends. Donna's family didn't attend church, but when her husband faced surgery for possible throat cancer she began to seek God.

We became good friends and she started coming to church with me. When she accepted Christ, I wanted to help her grow in faith and attain a vital, living relationship with God. I decided to apply the principles I'd learned and become Donna's mentor.

A TEACHER

The mentor's first role is that of a teacher: giving instructions, explanations, and guidance. At this stage, the mentor models a process and the beginner observes and asks questions.

I'll never forget the first question Donna asked me: "What do you think of reincarnation?"

I answered that one and many, many more as we spent time together almost daily, talking on the phone, drinking coffee while our sons played, going shopping. I told her how to know you're born again, showed her where to find passages in the Bible, advised her about decisions she had to make, and prayed aloud for her. But most important, I tried to use the way I lived and the Christian lifestyle I modeled to teach Donna as much as my words did. The knowledge that she was observing my life kept me on my knees.

A COACH

The second role a mentor fulfills is that of a coach. She still plays the leading role, but it's time for the disciple to get into the game. The responsibility for growth begins to shift. At this stage the mentor says, "Now you do it and I'll observe."

I knew it was time for my role to change when Donna joined the women's Bible study I led. As we proceeded through the lessons, I became her coach, standing back to watch and cheer as Donna acted. She soon grew confident in her ability to read the Scriptures and began contributing more and more to the discussions.

We still spent a lot of time talking together. But now instead of answering all her questions, I showed Donna where to look in the Bible and encouraged her to read it herself. Instead of advising her what to do, I explained God's principles and helped her decide. I no longer did all the praying; we began to pray together.

A COLLABORATOR

Gradually, the mentor's role shifts to that of a collaborator. Now the two people share responsibility for growth equally. They resolve questions and problems together in a give-and-take relationship, with the mentor's experience serving as a safeguard against the beginner's mistakes.

I watched Donna's faith grow quickly as God worked in her life. Her husband's tumor turned out to be benign. When her entire family began to worship regularly at our church, my mentoring role changed again. More and more, I encouraged Donna to go directly to God for answers to her questions or for guidance and direction in her life. I served as a collaborator, someone to discuss things with, and as her safety net, affirming her decisions. After four years, the mentoring process had helped Donna become nearly self-sufficient.

A SPONSOR

In teaching, the mentor's role changes to sponsor when she introduces the beginner to the broader professional community, giving her the opportunity to network with others and exposing her to additional resources such as organizations and seminars. The mentor also serves as an advocate, recommending the disciple for positions of responsibility.

Donna's enthusiastic, take-charge personality merged well with her deep spiritual hunger. Soon she began reaching out to others—befriending an unmarried co-worker who was pregnant and counseling her brother with his troubled marriage. In my new role as sponsor, I led Donna to the resources she needed to deepen her spiritual walk and to help others. I recommended books and seminars and introduced her to outstanding Christian role models and resources in our church and community. The responsibility for her spiritual growth was almost entirely hers; I merely provided a "nudge" from time to time.

A COUNSELOR

The mentor's final role is that of a counselor. The apprenticeship is nearly complete. The disciple now assumes full responsibility for continued growth but the mentor remains available to serve as a counselor and friend.

As time passed, Donna became very active in our church. When she learned that our annual women's retreat might be canceled due to lack of leadership, she volunteered to serve as chairwoman.

"We have to have a retreat!" she exclaimed. "There's someone at work I want to invite!"

As a member of the committee, I was one of Donna's advisers, but she provided the leadership. Her deep concern for her unsaved friend, coupled with her fresh insights as a growing Christian, equipped her to plan a retreat that blessed everyone who attended.

A few months after the women's retreat, my husband accepted a job offer in another state. My family and I would have to move. When the time came to find someone to lead the Bible study I'd started, I recommended Donna.

I felt satisfied that I'd done more for Donna than provide crisis intervention and a shoulder to lean on. In my role as mentor, I'd helped prepare her "for works of service, so that the body of Christ may be built up until we all reach unity in the faith and in the knowledge of the Son of God and become mature" (Ephesians 4:12-13). We'd reached the final goal of discipleship: Donna was no longer dependent on me, her mentor, but on the Lord.

A MATURE CHRISTIAN

During this time Gail also grew in her relationship with the Lord, once I began to mentor her. She required more urging than Donna as we progressed from one stage to the next. But, like a mother bird, I gently pushed Gail out of her comfortable nest. I taught her to keep a prayer journal, recording her growth and God's answers to prayers, and I encouraged her to teach a Sunday school class. Her gentle, trusting nature made her one of the best-loved teachers. Gradually, she became more dependent on God and less dependent on me.

Gail and I stood on my front lawn the day the real estate agent put a "for sale" sign on our house. "I'm going to pray that the Lord will send me another neighbor who's a mature Christian," Gail said.

"I don't think God will do that," I smiled.

"Why not?"

"Because I have a feeling He's going to send someone who will need a mature Christian neighbor like you!"[2]

———————◆———————

Stage	Definition	Possible activities	Relationship
Teacher	Mentor models a process and gives direct help; disciple observes and asks questions	Demonstrate how to read Scripture; pray aloud for disciple; model Christian lifestyle	Disciple is dependent on mentor
Coach	Mentor observes and directs as disciple practices new tasks	Encourage Bible study; pray with disciple; help disciple make decisions based on biblical principles	Disciple is 25 percent independent of mentor
Collaborator	Mentor and disciple work together cooperatively in give-and-take relationship	Discuss Scripture together; encourage a prayer journal; encourage disciple to seek God's direction	Disciple is 50 percent independent of mentor
Sponsor	Mentor introduces disciple to resources and wider network; mentor sponsors disciple for areas of ministry	Recommend books, organizations, and seminars for independent study; help disciple find and use gifts in ministry	Disciple is 75 percent independent of mentor
Counselor	Disciple functions independently; mentor advises and provides perspective	Help set long-range spiritual goals; advise disciple as he or she mentors others	Disciple is independent of mentor

ABOUT THE AUTHOR: Lynn Austin is a freelance writer and homemaker. She also sits on the editorial board of *Profile*, the journal of the Chicago Christian Women's Conference. One little-known fact about Lynn is her love of archaeology. She has spent a summer on a dig in Israel and looks forward to going back sometime.

QUESTIONS FOR REFLECTION

1. What keeps a mentor from changing roles with a mentoree?
2. What other roles can a mentor play in the life of a mentoree?

▶ TIPS FOR DISCIPLING

Mentoring New Disciplers

by Karen H. Whiting

The people who discipled me offered constant encouragement and invaluable input. Here's how you can receive the kind of information that will make you a better discipler and dispense information that will make your friend a better disciple.

Consider who encouraged you as a discipler. That person undoubtedly helped you persevere and succeed in discipling others. Now it's your turn to share what God has given you. Here are some pointers on mentoring aspiring disciplers:

Listen to the reasons they want to disciple others. Help them set and define goals. Listen for enthusiastic comments. Note what your friends enjoy, and feed that enthusiasm. Help the person you're discipling find a ministry outlet that matches his or her interest. Encourage that person to look for the right target audience: teens, young men, or families.

Share your start. You can instill hope by telling of your successes and struggles. Sharing your good and bad times in discipling may protect new disciplers from future discouragement.

Find talents. Identify each person's expertise based on life experiences, hobbies, and gifting. Discuss ways to use these as a bridge to reach others.

Celebrate first successes. Invite new disciplers to call and celebrate their success in discipling someone. Also, invite them to share their difficulties. Discuss those problems with them, and help them decide what to do next.

Be supportive. Listen with your eyes. Read emotions and respond accordingly. If you see signs of stress or frustration, for example, slow down or give a hug. New disciplers are sensitive and vulnerable. If they're insecure, the wrong words may discourage them forever.

Look for positive comments to make. Pay attention to complaints and brainstorm with your friends for solutions. You prepare your friends to disciple others when you help them find answers to problems. Keep a list of their questions and your responses. Follow up to see what helped. Make notes in case others ask similar questions.

Lend your resources. Discuss how tapes, magazines, and books have helped you. Have them keep index cards handy. When a verse or inspiring thought comes up, jot it down, and then pass it on. Make lists of reference, tapes, and magazines that help you grow. In addition, list resources that have equipped you as a discipler. Start a resource center of your own, or work through the church library to provide resources that encourage disciples and disciplers.

Interact with other disciplers at your church, at neighboring churches, on the Internet, or at conferences. Support and encourage one another by sharing your struggles and successes.

Do a walk-through. Walk through a typical week of discipling. Explain the process of prayer, Bible study, and other activities that are part of being a discipler. Discuss how you blend these commitments with the rest of your life, work, and relationships.

Share your inspiration. Tell what keeps you motivated and how you avoid over-commitment. Share the special Scriptures, devotions, or prayer methods that inspire your discipling.[3]

DESCRIPTION OF A DISCIPLE

LESSON PLAN

- Have two people share from personal devotional times.
- Review John 15:8 and other verses memorized to date.
- Discuss the Bible study "Description of a Disciple."
- Discuss the article "Principles of Selection."
- Continue to identify potential disciples and pray for them. Have members in the cluster group tell a little about the individuals they are thinking of talking to about a discipling relationship.
- Discuss the probable booklet the group—or members in the group—will be using in their discipling efforts. Refer to the Discipling Resources in appendix A (page 216).
- Discuss how to recruit someone into a discipling relationship.
- Discuss Tips for Discipling: "Finding the Right Person to Disciple."

ASSIGNMENT FOR SESSION 4: MINISTERING LIFE-TO-LIFE

- Prepare the Bible study "Ministering Life-to-Life."
- Read the article "Mentoring Others."
- Continue personal devotional times.
- Memorize 1 Thessalonians 2:7-8.
- Review previous verses daily.
- Read Tips for Discipling: "Guidelines and Checklist for the One-to-One Discipler."

GROUP PRAYER REQUESTS

▶ BIBLE STUDY

DESCRIPTION OF A DISCIPLE

KEY ISSUES
- What's a New Testament disciple?
- What's the role of a discipler?
- What's the core content for the discipling process?

The Term *Disciple* is used more than two hundred fifty times in the Gospels and the book of Acts. Considering that Luke, discipled by Paul, wrote Acts around A.D. 65, that term wasn't used only in the ministry of Christ, but was part of the language and understanding of the first-century church.

Our quest is to understand what Jesus meant by *disciple,* because it's His term that's binding on the church throughout history. We're not free to make up our own definition or use what's popular either in Jesus' day or our own. The search for the meaning of *disciple* and *discipleship* isn't simple. It won't be found in a short three- or four-word definition. The search for its true meaning, although not easy, is essential in understanding our mission.

Explain why you agree or disagree with the following statement: "Every believer is a disciple of Jesus Christ."

In order to understand what Jesus meant by a disciple, we must look at how He used the word and described it. *Disciple* is easier to describe than to define, as a precise definition is difficult to find in Scripture. The simplest definition of a disciple is found in Matthew 4:19 when Jesus said, "Follow me, and I will make you fishers of men." A disciple is a follower of Christ at the most fundamental level. A disciple is one who follows and consequently becomes like the One being followed. Discipleship was more than adhering to a set of teachings or principles: it was a relationship of transformation.

In the Gospels, Jesus described what He meant by discipleship. Because He hasn't rescinded these traits or characteristics, it's imperative that we understand and adhere to what He meant if we're to become involved in making *His* disciples. Using these clear definitions, we can conclude that discipleship may be more than this but it can't be less.

First of all, it is clear that, if we would make disciples, we should be disciples . . . To plan on making disciples, we need to know what one is and how people become disciples. We need to know these things by personal experience, as did the first generation of Jesus' people.[1]

DALLAS WILLARD

1. There are two main ways we can describe the concept of being a disciple. One is "are my disciples" and the other is "can't be my disciple." Meditate on the following verses and make observations regarding the traits or characteristics of a disciple of Jesus. Use the accompanying questions to stimulate your observations.

Scripture	What is stated as a quality of a disciple?	What does each quality, or trait, mean to you?	What are the implications in the life of a disciple?
Luke 6:40			
Luke 14:25-27			
Luke 14:33			
John 8:31-32			
John 13:34-35			
John 15:8			

2. What do the following verses teach about disciplemaking?
Matthew 4:19

Acts 13:52

Romans 15:14

2 Timothy 2:2

3. Jesus pointed out that when one has been fully trained he "will be like his teacher" (Luke 6:40). In the Greek language, the heart of the word *disciple* means "learner." Is training the same as teaching? Explain.

BUILDING LIFE ON A SOLID FOUNDATION

Therefore everyone who hears these words of mine and puts them into practice is like a wise man who built his house on the rock. The rain came down, the streams rose, and the winds blew and beat against that house; yet it did not fall, because it had its foundation on the rock. But everyone who hears these words of mine and does not put them into practice is like a foolish man who built his house on sand. (Matthew 7:24-27)

4a. List similarities and differences between the two houses in Matthew 7:24-27.

4b. How is "teaching them" different from "teaching them to obey" as used in Matthew 28:20?

DEFINING DISCIPLESHIP

5. Writing a concise definition of Christian discipleship is indeed difficult. Read the following statements and then, using your study so far, write out your own description or definition of a disciple of Christ. Please take time to review what you've studied so far to wrestle with this question.

- *The American Heritage Dictionary* (Houghton Mifflin, 1985): "One who subscribes to the teaching of a master and assists in spreading them; an active adherent, as of a movement or philosophy. Often disciple—one of the companions of Christ."
- Christopher B. Adsit: "A disciple is a person-in-process who is eager to learn and apply the truths that Jesus Christ teaches him, which will result in ever-deepening commitments to a Christ-like lifestyle."
- Ron Bennett: "Discipleship is the proactive process of growing in godliness (Christlikeness) through the exercise of spiritual disciplines."

- Howard Hendricks: "A disciple is a learner, who is following Jesus Christ, and whose life is marked by obedience, love, and fruitfulness."
- Chuck Strittmatter: "A disciple is a devoted follower of Jesus Christ who lives and thinks according to the Word of God."
- Eastbourne, England, Consultation on Discipleship (Fall 1999): "While there are valid differences of perspective on what constitutes discipleship, we define Christian discipleship as a process that takes place within accountable relationships over a period of time for the purpose of bringing believers to spiritual maturity in Christ. Biblical examples suggest that discipleship is both relational and intentional, both position and process."
- George Barna: "We might define discipleship as becoming a complete and competent follower of Jesus Christ. It is about the intentional training of people who voluntarily submit to the lordship of Jesus Christ and who want to become imitators of Christ in every thought, word and deed. On the basis of teaching, training, experiences, relationships and accountability, we become transformed into the likeness of Jesus Christ."[2]

Your definition: A disciple is:

HOW PEOPLE BECOME DISCIPLES

After proclaiming the Message in Derbe and establishing a strong core of disciples, they retraced their steps to Lystra, then Iconium, and then Antioch. (Acts 14:21, MSG)

The primary characteristic of a disciple of Jesus is that he or she becomes "like" Jesus (Luke 6:40). When a person comes to faith in Christ, God begins a process of helping that person become more and more like Jesus (see Romans 8:28-29).

Obviously, becoming like Jesus is a pretty tall order. How does it happen? The New Testament gives us a process that involves three sets of persons:

- One part only God (Father, Son, and Holy Spirit) can play.
- One part others play in our lives.
- One part only we can play.

GOD'S PART IN MAKING DISCIPLES

6. Because God wants us to be transformed into the likeness of His Son, He's at work to bring about necessary changes. What do the following verses teach about God's role in developing disciples?

John 15:1-2

Romans 8:28-29

2 Corinthians 3:18

Philippians 1:6

Philippians 2:12-13

Colossians 3:10 says that once we come into a relationship with Christ, we're being "renewed" according to the image of the One who created us. Another word for *renewed* is *renovated*.

Renovating is getting rid of, or correcting, what's old and damaged, and returning something to a state where it's like new. When God begins a renovation project, He's committed to finishing it. God will do the work that He set out to do (see Philippians 1:6).

OTHERS' PART IN MAKING DISCIPLES

My children, with whom I am again in labor until Christ is formed in you . . . (Galatians 4:19, NASB)

7a. In the following verse, how did Paul describe his role in making disciples? (Note the verbs and what they mean.) "We proclaim him, admonishing and teaching everyone with all wisdom, so that we may present everyone perfect in Christ. To this end I labor, struggling with all his energy, which so powerfully works in me" (Colossians 1:28-29).

7b. What does the "labor" that others do look like in the following verses?

Philippians 1:1-3

Philippians 1:9-11

Philippians 3:17

1 Thessalonians 2:7-12

1 Timothy 4:10-13

2 Timothy 2:2

For the purpose of this study, we're calling a person who gives focused labor to help others become like Jesus a "discipler." A discipler is involved in the work of praying, modeling, and instructing. He or she is a disciple of Jesus Christ actively sharing faith and discipling others; someone who is involved in the Great Commission of Matthew 28:19-20.

> We have to come to terms with the fact that we cannot become those who "hear and do" without specific training for it. The training may be to some extent self-administered, but more than that will always be needed. It is something that must be made available to us by those already farther along the path.
>
> That clearly was the understanding of Jesus for His people. Training in Christlikeness is a responsibility they have for those who enter their number.
>
> DALLAS WILLARD

THE INDIVIDUAL DISCIPLE'S PART

8a. Review Philippians 2:12-13, where God is doing His part. What is our part?

8b. Review the chart you developed in question 1. Record the things the Lord said we must *do* if we want to be His disciples.

PROFILE OF A DISCIPLE

If a discipler makes disciples in partnership with the Holy Spirit, then there must be a body of training that, when mastered, makes someone a disciple. These essentials should be simple, identifiable, realistic, and achievable in some time frame.

The passages from question 1 provide a basis for understanding what Christ taught regarding being His disciple. The following profile of the four aspects of a disciple's life summarizes Jesus' teaching:

- Conviction (John 8:31-32)—the mind
- Character (John 13:34-35)—the heart
- Competence (John 15:8)—the hands
- Commitment (Luke 14:25-27)—the feet[3]

A maturing disciple grows in all four aspects—not just in some. While some aspects are more difficult and take more time to develop than others, both disciples and disciplers develop in all four.

The Navigators' Wheel Illustration (at right) provides another practical framework that demonstrates the process of making disciples. The six components that make up this illustration capture the basic essentials of discipleship and provide a practical reference point for understanding the profile of a disciple. (For a further explanation of this illustration, see The Navigators' 2:7 Series *Growing Strong in God's Family*.)

If the essence of discipleship is being like Christ (see Luke 6:40; Romans 8:29), then our part starts with becoming a student of the Master. We need to know Him intimately.

In the early 1400s, a priest known as Thomas á Kempis was in charge of training the novice monks of the monastery at Mount St. Agnes in the Netherlands. In 1441, he wrote down much of what he taught the men he discipled. For the past five hundred years, his writing has been published under the title *Of the Imitation of Christ*. His book starts this way:

> "He that follows Me shall not walk in darkness," says the Lord. These are the words of Christ, by which we are urged to imitate His life and virtues, if we wish to be truly enlightened and freed from all blindness of heart. Therefore, let it be our chief business to meditate upon the life of Jesus Christ. . . . If you would understand Christ's words fully and taste them truly, you must strive to form your whole life after His pattern.

MODELS OF DISCIPLESHIP

9a. What other models have you seen that help describe a disciple?

9b. Using a model described in this study or a model of your own, identify four or five actions or characteristics of a disciple. You might want to use words that finish one or both of these statements: (1) "A disciple of Christ will . . . " (2) "A disciple of Christ is someone who . . . "

Principles of Selection

by Ron Bennett

IN A BUSY SOCIETY, in order to disciple others, we need to employ some kind of criteria to figure out which people to minister to. Discipling others is intentional, focused, and personal. Each discipler has very limited time, emotional energy, and spiritual availability.

Selection is a normal part of life. By definition, selection means to choose in preference to another or others; to pick out; to make a choice; to discriminate. We're constantly selecting and being selected. Selection means that out of a variety of options, we can only utilize a few. It recognizes that the discipler has limitations that affect his or her effectiveness.

Most of the Old Testament is the account of how God worked His purposes through the nation He selected out of all nations. Jesus applied the principle of selection in choosing the Twelve He would call apostles. The Gospels are mainly an account of the training of the Twelve for the future of the gospel ministry. Since Jesus didn't heal everyone during His ministry, He was constantly making decisions about people He'd interact with.

The principle of selection assumes an objective, options, some criteria, and an appeal.

THE OBJECTIVE

First, selection must have an objective, a reason, a desired goal. Mark 3:14 states that Jesus was clear and intentionally chose the Twelve to train them and send them out to preach. Christ's call to the fishermen in Matthew 4:19 includes an objective. In order to select, we must first know what we're selecting people for.

When Paul told Timothy to select key people, he laid out the purpose: "Who will also be qualified to teach others" (2 Timothy 2:2). Timothy was to select people in order to further the process of spiritual multiplication.

We have a variety of spiritual reasons to select people. We'll assume that the objective for disciplers is to help believers become more mature by helping them develop a strong foundation of faith and discipleship. This objective needs to be clear to the discipler as well as to the potential disciple.

I express the objective in terms that the new believer can understand and find motivational. It may be a long-term goal for a student to be able to understand algebra, but for the child in second grade, learning the multiplication tables is a worthy goal. Learning how to express spiritual maturity in terms that the new believer can comprehend is critical for disciplers.

For example, I might tell the new Christian I'm going to help him connect with God on a daily basis by spending time in the Scriptures and then praying. The goal is to establish a quiet time, but it is spoken in language the new believer can relate to.

OPTIONS

Selecting assumes that there are more possibilities than realities. Therefore, I work from a pool of options.

Jesus ministered for more than a year in the public domain before He selected the Twelve. He established Himself, His credibility, and His agenda before He concentrated on a few. He developed His reputation as a teacher, as a worker of miracles, as the Son of Man, and as laying claim to being the Messiah. People saw Him as having something to offer those He selected.

Selection requires that we establish ourselves as disciples with a solid walk with God. From this platform of credibility we then can select people for discipling life-to-life. Selection requires that we establish this credibility before a variety of people, and then we can select some to disciple. This credibility before others may come from teaching a class or serving in a ministry. It comes as we live out our discipleship in practical ways before others.

Where do you have an "insider connection" for selection? Where do you have contact with young believers who've observed your manner of life and respect your maturity? Church? Work? Neighborhood? Identify the networks where God has already provided environments for selection. Who in those networks might be possibilities for your investment of discipling?

CRITERIA

The next part of selection—assuming that you're clear in your purpose and have identified a pool to choose from—is to establish sorting criteria. Why select one person over another? What would make one person a better investment of your time and energy over others?

Jesus doesn't give us a list of criteria that He used in selecting the Twelve. However, we can make some observations from looking at the people. For the most part they were from the common strata of life, not elite or influential. It was exactly that observation that made their ministry in Acts so outstanding to the leaders in Jerusalem: "When they saw the courage of Peter and John and realized that they were unschooled, ordinary men, they were astonished and they took note that these men had been with Jesus" (Acts 4:13).

When God assigned the prophet Samuel to select the king to replace Saul, He sent him to the house of Jesse. "I have chosen one of his sons to be king," God told him (1 Samuel 16:1). As Samuel looked at the eldest son, Eliab, he thought, *Wow! Great king material.* But God rejected each of the seven older sons as He gave Samuel (and us) a principle that should guide us when we select the people we want to disciple: "But the LORD said to Samuel, 'Do not consider his appearance or his height, for I have rejected him. The LORD does not look at the things man looks at. Man looks at the outward appearance, but the LORD looks at the heart'" (1 Samuel 16:7).

We can make two observations from this statement. The first is that God's priority is on the internal, the character . . . the heart. External characteristics are irrelevant compared to the inner heart. The second is that we can't observe the heart; we can see only externals. Even when we try to observe the quality of the heart, we're limited to outward indicators and need God's guidance.

There are three critical qualities for selecting potential disciples.

1. FAITHFUL

Paul gives Timothy the criteria for selecting people to focus on: "Pass on what you heard from me—the whole congregation saying Amen!—to reliable leaders who are competent to teach others" (2 Timothy 2:2, MSG).

The key choice was to be made on reliability, or faithfulness. Paul was concerned with the inner character rather than external looks or influence. Faithfulness primarily means that someone is fundamentally a person full of faith, and secondarily that he or she can be counted on. Possibly, Paul had in mind the teaching of Jesus when he said, "Whoever can be trusted with very little can also be trusted with much, and whoever is dishonest with very little will also be dishonest with much. So if you have not been trustworthy in handling worldly wealth, who will trust you with true riches? And if you have not been trustworthy with someone else's property, who will give you property of your own?" (Luke 16:10-12).

2. RESPONSIVE

Those Jesus spent continued time with were demonstrated learners. The disciples were often slow to catch on, but they were seeking truth. They wanted to know. They asked questions. Even in the initial days when Jesus was introduced as the Lamb of God, some of the early followers asked the superficial question, "Where are you staying?" Still, even to this question, Jesus gave the invitation, "Come and see." He didn't condemn, judge, or hinder them.

Look for people who want to learn. As we've already seen, the root meaning of the word *disciple* means "learner." If people are to become mature disciples, they must be learners. There must be the hunger to know, grow, and understand. Their lives may not yet reflect sainthood, but they want to learn. It's been said that three things are extremely difficult to do: climb a ladder leaning toward you, kiss a person leaning away from you, and disciple someone who is not leaning toward learning.

Richard is a successful doctor with a heart for discipling. His ministry focuses on young interns at his hospital. Everyone is busy. Most work seventy to eighty hours per week—typical of that profession. "I know they're busy," Richard says, "so I offer to meet with them at 5 A.M. Even interns aren't busy at that hour!"

3. AVAILABLE

Availability doesn't mean people are unoccupied or idle. Jesus wasn't afraid to select and recruit busy people who were successfully and actively pursuing their goals. To respond to Jesus, people had to count the costs, leave what they were doing, and choose another (higher) priority. Don't be afraid to choose active, busy people. You're looking for people who will make time to learn what you have to teach. They'll make it a priority. They'll take discipleship seriously and focus on it.

Discipling life-to-life requires contact, which means availability. It may mean a lot of flexibility on the part of the discipler, but time together interacting around the Word is essential. In a society that values being busy—even with good things like work, family, and church—discipling others life-to-life will require an adjustment of schedules, priorities, and focus.

Even when we're comfortable with our criteria, our selection should always include waiting on God to lead in confirming the people you should invest in. Jesus spent time in prayer—"spent the night praying to God" (Luke 6:12)—before choosing the Twelve. Jesus wanted to invest in those God had chosen. In John 17, Jesus prays with confidence for the Twelve because "they were yours; you gave them to me" (verse 6).

Discipling others includes the role of a steward. We take what God entrusts to us and make a contribution. We're servants, not owners. Knowing that God confirms this ministry between two people helps us through disappointing times when progress seems slow or nonexistent. Jesus had times when He thought the disciples would never get it. And so will we. The patience of the parent comes from knowing that children are a gift placed in our care for a season.

Selection doesn't mean that others aren't important. Jesus did many things with a large number of people but He focused on a few. In addition to the Twelve, there were the seventy, the five hundred, and the other individuals that Jesus touched along the way. Still, His strategy was concentrating on a few selected people so that they in turn could reach larger numbers.

RECRUITING THROUGH AN APPEAL

An essential part of the selection process ends with an appeal to the person you're recruiting. You give an invitation and the person must respond. We may have the right life-to-life to offer, they need it, and God is in it, but if they're not convinced of all of this, it will never fly.

The potential disciple must know that the mission is to focus on following Christ and not the discipler. The goal is to sojourn together as disciples of Christ, not as disciples of the church or group or another person.

We should recruit to a specific agenda and expectations. "I would like to disciple you for the rest of your life" could be threatening to a new believer. On the other hand, "I would like to help you understand some fundamental concepts in your journey with Christ by going through this study series" could be more attractive. The potential disciple then knows what's covered, what's expected, and some kind of time frame.

The potential disciple needs to know that you know where you're going and how you intend to get there. You can make adjustments along the way, but setting the parameters gives the potential disciple a sense of confidence and security.

How I recruit depends on where the people are in their maturity. If they're very young spiritually, I keep it very short-term and simple. I may ask them to meet with me for a series of five lessons. If they like it, we can do more. If they're more mature, I'll make the offer more comprehensive by lengthening both the time and the material or topics covered. One advantage of working with a short, specific time frame is that it gives you, the discipler, a point of evaluation to decide if you want to continue. You may decide that you've helped someone as far as you or the disciple can go at this time.

Recruiting is simply your way of getting the agenda up front and allowing the person the option to accept it or not.

In summary, the reality is that selection is necessary. It means we have objectives to give the potential person to be discipled, we've identified people from the pool of our spheres of influence, and we've evaluated the people based on criteria of faithfulness, responsiveness, and availability. Finally, we've recruited them through an appeal. Paul says in 1 Corinthians 11:1, "Follow my example, as I follow the example of Christ."

QUESTIONS FOR REFLECTION

1. What is your network of credibility for selection?
2. What are the issues you're facing when selecting a person to invest your life in?

▶ TIPS FOR DISCIPLING

Finding the Right Person to Disciple

by Becky Brodin

"You know what, Kathy? I think you're ready to disciple someone."

"Really?" she responded, blinking in surprise. "Do you think I could do it?"

I'd been discipling Kathy for more than a year. She had a sensitive heart, a deep desire to know the Lord, and an eagerness to learn. I knew that if she could help a younger believer grow, her understanding of discipleship would soar.

Then she asked, "Who should I disciple?"

That's a good question. A notice on a bulletin board at church probably won't work since many believers don't even know what discipleship is. I realized this a few years ago when I asked a woman in my Sunday school class to meet for coffee to talk about her spiritual growth. She looked at me like a deer staring into headlights, but she was willing, and we began to meet weekly. Several weeks later, she confessed she initially thought I wanted to scold her! She was unfamiliar with one-to-one discipleship. Because many people we might want to disciple are similar to Kathy, we have to take the initiative to begin a discipling relationship.

Finding someone to disciple requires three things:

- involvement with people,
- knowing what to look for,
- and a willingness to take initiative.

POOLS OF PEOPLE

To find someone to disciple, you need to be involved with people.

In our culture, this usually happens in some kind of small group, such as a Bible study or a Sunday school class.

When Jesus selected His disciples, He didn't run His finger down a list of names in the Galilee phone book and pick people at random. Luke 5 and 6 describe how He established Himself in the area. He preached, healed, ministered, and soon had a group of people following Him. Then, after a night of prayer, "he called his disciples to him and chose twelve of them, whom he also designated apostles" (Luke 6:13). Jesus was involved with people before He connected with them individually. They knew Him, and He knew them.

Kathy participated regularly in a Sunday school class at her church and co-led a small-group Bible study. I also knew she was actively building relationships. The stage was set for Kathy to look for someone to disciple.

THE RIGHT STUFF

What an interesting mix of men Jesus chose as His disciples! Laborers, political zealots, educated professionals. He looked past their personalities and professions for deeper qualities. While Kathy wasn't selecting apostles, she did need some criteria to help her evaluate the suitability of those she was considering.

Years ago, a wise mentor told me to be patient with this step of the process. He suggested looking for someone who is hungry to grow and instructed me to wait and watch for four to six months before I approached someone. When I asked him how I could tell, he assured me I would know. He was right. Those who wanted to grow:

- were committed to fellowship,
- studied on their own,
- and took the initiative to develop relationships.

Though this list may seem subjective, it's a good place to start. It will help you identify those who are interested in spiritual growth and those who will follow through.

Kathy had been involved in her groups for several months. When I asked her who seemed spiritually hungry, she named two people from her Bible study. She wanted to connect with both of them immediately. But I convinced her to pray about it, following Jesus' example. After she'd done so, she was ready to take the next step.

TAKING THE PLUNGE

A discipling relationship is unique. It's personal. And it can be demanding, intense, time consuming, and life changing. Launching such a relationship requires initiative and honesty.

Luke 5:27-28 describes how Jesus recruited Matthew: "After this, Jesus went out and saw a tax collector by the name of Levi sitting at his tax booth. 'Follow me,' Jesus said to him, and Levi got up, left everything and followed him." The word *follower* in the Greek describes someone who seeks to be like his teacher, a companion who is "going in the same way." When Jesus called His disciples to follow Him, they knew what it meant. Whenever people chose to follow a particular teacher, they often left their jobs and current way of life to do so.

When Kathy and I talked about how to begin her relationship with someone she wanted to disciple, I suggested that she clearly describe the discipleship process. What she was asking of these women would require a commitment of time and purpose. I urged Kathy to be honest about it all. Kathy and I had begun our relationship the same way.

ON THE LOOKOUT

Kathy met with both people for more than two years. Then each of them began discipling others. But Kathy didn't stop there. She continues to watch for people who are hungry to grow, takes the initiative to relate to them, and invites them into a unique adventure of one-to-one discipleship.[4]

MINISTERING LIFE-TO-LIFE

LESSON PLAN

- Discuss highlights from personal devotional times.
- Review 1 Thessalonians 2:7-8.
- *Important:* Return to a discussion of "Rules for the Journey" on pages 20-21. Evaluate and make changes accordingly.
- Discuss the Bible study "Ministering Life-to-Life."
- Discuss the article "Mentoring Others."
- Share the names of those that each in your cluster group will be discipling. Record their names on the worksheet on page 219 and spend some time praying for them by name.
- Share concerns and issues that aren't yet resolved as the new disciplers move into the ministry of discipling. Pray for responsive hearts and learner attitudes.
- Discuss issues related to recruiting people to a discipling relationship.
- Discuss Tips for Discipling: "Guidelines and Checklist for the One-to-One Discipler."
- Note that if you are following the Discipling Syllabus (page 17), you'll change your cluster group meetings to once per month (instead of weekly) beginning with your next meeting.

ASSIGNMENT FOR SESSION 5: FOLLOW ME

- Prepare "Follow Me" Bible study.
- Read the article "Questions I'd Ask Before Following Jesus."
- Memorize Matthew 4:19-20.
- Continue personal devotional times.
- Begin your mentoring with a growing disciple.
- Read the Tips for Discipling: "Doing a Life-to-Life Session."

GROUP PRAYER REQUESTS

► BIBLE STUDY

MINISTERING LIFE-TO-LIFE

KEY ISSUES
- What is life-to-life ministry?
- What are the core components of an effective life-to-life ministry?
- What are some considerations for me as a discipler?
- What are some unique values and qualities of giving someone focused attention?

Discipling others implies one person affecting or influencing another. Discipling others is a relational ministry of helping another person become mature in Christ. So how is it done? What are the relational dynamics that make for biblical disciplemaking?

"Life-to-life" is a way to express the relational concept of one life personally touching another. It involves not only intentionally passing on knowledge and skill but values, heart, and passion. It's more than transferring concepts or principles.

Many of us can remember the life-changing impact teachers or coaches had on our lives when we were touched by their love of the material or sport even more than by their instruction. Their passion may have been the catalyst that launched a particular career or field of study. We may not remember a single lecture or pep talk, but we were touched forever by their life message.

FOR REFLECTION

Write a brief paragraph on who's been a personal model and motivator to you (teacher, coach, friend, parent, and so forth), how you were influenced, and how it made you feel.

The term *life-to-life* isn't used in Scripture but the concept is there consistently. Examples of words found in the Bible that convey the concept of life-to-life are *pattern, example, model, imitate, follow me,* and *watch me*. When the term *life-to-life* is used in *The Adventure of Discipling Others,* here's what it means:

- Two or more people in an intentional, purposeful learning experience where each is committed to Christian discipleship, transparency, and full maturity.
- The relational dynamic between two people that enables the transfer of the knowledge, heart, vision, and skill for becoming mature and wholehearted followers of Christ.

LIFE-TO-LIFE CASE STUDY

Life-to-life is more than being together—or even sharing common activities. When the writers of the Bible use a term for ministry that describes something deeper than simply passing on knowledge, they use terms like *pattern, example, model,* and *imitate.* "Life-to-life" implies both someone modeling and someone observing.

Imitate—To mimic; to do what is seen. To behave in the same manner as someone else. To call attention to a comparison even when no conscious mimicking is in mind.[1]

Example—An equivalent to "be obedient."[2]

1a. Meditate on the life-to-life example of Paul and Timothy summarized in 2 Timothy 3:10-17. Use the following questions to guide your observations about what is said or implied. What did the discipler model?

What was the imitator (new disciple) to do? To become?

How did Paul's "way of life" example compare to teaching or instruction?

Some communication experts estimate that actions are six times more powerful than words. Spiritual modeling and imitation require core relational interactions with your new disciple that some refer to as "relational dynamics." Different disciplers have different emphases, depending on spiritual modeling and their personalities. Some of these dynamics are listed on page 72.

1b. Paul met Timothy in Acts 16:1-5. Underline what you see of life-to-life discipleship.

He came to Derbe and then to Lystra, where a disciple named Timothy lived, whose mother was a Jewess and a believer, but whose father was a Greek. The brothers at

Lystra and Iconium spoke well of him. Paul wanted to take him along on the journey, so he circumcised him because of the Jews who lived in that area, for they all knew that his father was a Greek. As they traveled from town to town, they delivered the decisions reached by the apostles and elders in Jerusalem for the people to obey. So the churches were strengthened in the faith and grew daily in numbers. (Acts 16:1-5)

1c. Read the brief definitions below and make observations on how you see them demonstrated in the case study of Paul and Timothy in 2 Timothy 3:10-17.

Intentionality: action by design; purposeful; relating based on decision; modeling or imitating is done on purpose

Modeling: what is demonstrated is to be imitated

Integration: consistency between what's taught and what's lived

Teachability: responsiveness to being taught; willingness to learn from another

Availability: making time to share, expose, and observe

Transparency: lives willingly open to be observed, imitated, shared, and changed

Equipping: character, ability, and skill can be learned by another

1d. What relational dynamics other than these listed above do you feel ought to be part of a life-to-life ministry? Why?

1e. Let's assume you're interviewing Paul for an article in *Jerusalem Today*. How do you think he would describe the term *life-to-life*?

LIFE-TO-LIFE GIVES FOCUSED ATTENTION

In a life-to-life ministry, the discipler places high value on the individual being discipled. A laser beam has to be focused very precisely to be of any value in surgery or to read CD-ROMs. The discipler needs focus that's intentional, intense, and in tune for good life-to-life to happen. Focused attention means meeting the needs of the individual—touching that person's life in relevant ways. It doesn't always mean, however, that you give attention in isolation. Jesus often focused on one individual in the context of others.

2a. How is a focus of attention demonstrated in the following passages?
   Matthew 16:13-20

   Luke 8:40-53

   Luke 19:1-10

Giving a new disciple focused attention means concentrating energy toward the person at the exclusion of other efforts. Think of it as a spiritual laser beam—or like playing with a child and giving 100 percent of your concentration by not doing other activities like watching TV or reading a magazine at the same time.

2b. How do the following verses involve one person using focused attention?
   Acts 20:31

   Colossians 1:28

2c. How might focused attention look when:
   Alone with one other person?

   In the context of a small group?

COACHING AND LIFE-TO-LIFE

Coaching is a form of life-to-life and involves focused attention. The coach—whether in sports, music, business, or spiritual maturity—observes, evaluates, instructs, models, and motivates. Coaching usually involves helping another person develop skills, abilities, knowledge, and confidence to perform a task better.

3a. What aspects of a superlative coach do you see in the following passages?

Deuteronomy 3:28

1 Samuel 14:6-7

Acts 20:28,31

Ephesians 4:11-13

1 Thessalonians 5:12-13

Titus 2:7-8

1 Peter 5:1-3

3b. Summarize what you think makes an effective spiritual coach.

According to William Barclay,

Paul contrasts the conduct of Timothy, his loyal disciple, with the conduct of the heretics who were doing their utmost to wreck the Church. The word we have translated *to be a disciple* includes so much that is beyond translation in any single English word. It is the Greek *parakolouthein* and literally means *to follow alongside*; but it is used with a magnificent width of meaning. It means to follow a person *physically*, to stick by him through thick and thin. It means to follow a person *mentally*, to attend diligently to his teaching and fully to understand the meaning of what he says. It means to follow a person *spiritually*, not only to understand what he says, but also to carry out his ideas and be the kind of person he wishes us to be. *Parakolouthein* is indeed the word for the disciple, for it includes the unwavering loyalty of the true comrade, the full understanding of the true scholar, and the complete obedience of the dedicated servant.

Paul goes on to list the things in which Timothy has been his disciple . . .

First, there is *teaching*. No man can teach what he does not know, and therefore before a man can teach Christ to others he must know him himself. When Carlyle's father was discussing the kind of minister his parish needed, he said: "What this parish needs is a man who knows Christ other than at secondhand." Real teaching is always born of real experience. There is *training*. The Christian life does not consist only in knowing something; it consists even more in being something. The task of the apostle is not only to tell men the truth; it is also to help them do it. The true leader gives training in living.

Second, he has an *aim in life*. Then, there is *faith*, and *patience*. The word here is *makrothumia*; as the Greeks used it, usually meant *patience with people*; not to grow irritable when they seem unteachable. There is *love*. This is God's attitude to men. Paul completes the story . . . by speaking of the quality of *endurance*. The Greek is *hupomone*, which means not a passive sitting down and bearing things but a triumphant facing of them so that even out of evil there can come good. It describes, not the spirit that *accepts* life, but the spirit that *masters* it.[3]

SUMMARY

4. What challenged you most from this study?

5. How would you describe a life-to-life ministry now?

6. What aspect of life-to-life do you need to apply to your disciplemaking ministry?

OPTIONAL, FOR FURTHER THOUGHT:
How would you contrast a life-to-life ministry with a "program" ministry?

Mentoring Others

by Larry Glabe

SKILLFUL SPIRITUAL PARENTING IS critical to help new believers grow by design rather than by default toward spiritual maturity. But few people experience this type of mentoring themselves.

In groups where I've taught on mentoring life-to-life, I often ask how many have personally had intentional individual help in their spiritual life. One of ten to one of twenty is the normal response. But even without personal models, the benefits of learning and ministering in this manner are so critical, it's worth the effort to learn. As more people begin to experience personal mentoring, the more models we have, the greater the potential for others to be touched by this style of ministry.

I'm using mentoring to describe a spiritual, personal, intentional, life-to-life ministry to others. I define mentoring as:

Getting excited about helping someone else become successful by being an example, sharing my experience, and passing on my expertise in an encouraging manner.

Mentoring has unique benefits. Mentoring has the ability to build a greater level of trust, respect, and depth between people. In a mentoring ministry, people are willing to raise issues that often remain hidden. When mentors and the people they're mentoring establish a deep level of trust, they become willing to expose their real questions, weaknesses, and problems.

Paul speaks of this task in 1 Corinthians 3:10: "According to the grace of God which was given to me, as a wise master builder I laid a foundation, and another is building upon it. But let each man be careful how he builds upon it."

A person reaching people is God's design for Kingdom influence and expansion. We can look at mentoring in light of the pattern, potential, process, and promise.

We read of the *pattern* in John 17 as Jesus reflects in prayer that He accomplished the work God gave Him to do. This work was different than His work on the cross. He's speaking of finished work. He was already done. You can summarize this work as:

1. He loved the world.
2. He taught the multitudes.
3. He gave himself to twelve people.

We read of the *potential* of life-to-life ministry in 2 Timothy 2:2. The four generations highlighted in this verse create a picture of a chain. Each generation becomes a separate link that holds the chain together. Will we become the last link in the chain or will we add other links? Will we leave a legend or a legacy?

Paul told Timothy to "entrust" to faithful people what was entrusted to him. The word *entrust* implies something of value to be passed on. Where does the value come from? Who gives it value? Paul or Timothy? It seems that the mentors establish the value and then pass it on to succeeding generations. We can often become complacent and devalue what's valuable and fail to pass on both the content and its worth. What do you need to pass on to others that God entrusts to you?

We see an illustration of the *process* in 1 Thessalonians, especially in chapter 2, where Paul identifies his ministry as a sharing of both the Word and his life. He became both a mother and a father to these new converts. As a result of our personality or experience, most of us tend to be stronger either in the role of being gentle, tender, and affectionate, or in the role of being an exhorter, encourager, and trainer. Life-to-life requires the ability to become both to those we mentor. Each personal encounter we have with a mentoree may require both roles.

God's *promises* are critical to sustain us in this personal ministry. Promises give us power, perspective, and perseverance. Personally, Isaiah 60:21-22 has been foundational for me over the years. I pray over it with my wife when we get discouraged, and we ask God to fulfill it. It reminds us that God is building the house and He's more interested than I am to see it accomplished.

Then will all your people be righteous and they will possess the land forever. They are the shoots I have planted, the work of my hands, for the display of my splendor. The least of you will become a thousand, the smallest a mighty nation. I am the LORD; in its time I will do this swiftly. (Isaiah 60:21-22)

THE PRACTICE

Truth never changes, but where people are in relationship to the truth does. As a spiritual mentor, it's helpful to have sound blueprints that help us guide young believers to truth.

SELECTION

The first important question is, Whom do we mentor? How do we decide who to invest personal time in? Jesus spent all night in prayer just prior to selecting the Twelve. He was confident from His prayer in John 17 that those He invested in were ones that God had given Him. We need to be confident that we're investing in those God gives us.

One grid I've used over the years to help me discern who to invest in is asking the question, "Do they have a heart for God, His Word, and people?" These three qualities are critical to becoming a link in the chain of spiritual reproduction. The people in question may not know a lot and they may have major obstacles to overcome, but if they demonstrate these three qualities, they become potential mentorees for me. I've found Isaiah 58:10 helpful for the process of selection for mentoring: "If you spend yourselves in behalf of the hungry and satisfy the needs of the oppressed, then your light will rise in the darkness, and your night will become like the noonday."

Finding those who are hungry is essential to investing my life. A number of ways exist for finding hungry people, but one way I do it is to, in a spiritual sense, lay food before people and see if they eat it. When I lead a small group or workshop, I look to see who seems to pick up on what I'm sharing and which men display hunger. It's easy to sense a "been there, done that" attitude or a "ho hum" response. Likewise, those who pick up on the Word, ask questions, or seem to reflect on it become potential mentorees.

VISION

Laying out a vision for growth is another practical part of a mentoring ministry. We need to establish the parameters of where we're going, how we're going to get there, and how long we're planning to take. Proverbs 29:18 reminds us, "Where there is no vision the people perish."

Describing where we're going is beneficial to both the mentor and mentoree. Having a roadmap that describes the process helps each person have a clearer understanding of what's expected. I use a diamond with four sides to illustrate four stages of spiritual maturity. I explain what each side means in terms of spiritual maturity and use it to paint the big picture. I also help the mentoree identify where he is in the process.

I also share the vision by referring to the Great Commission and the Great Commandment like a pair of glasses. There are two lenses but one vision. We don't walk with one eye covered;

instead we keep both eyes open and look ahead through both lenses at the same time. The Great Commission tells us what to do and the Great Commandment tells us what we are to become. Both are critical for maturity.

In establishing the vision for mentoring, the mentoree needs to answer two vital questions: (1) Do you want to grow spiritually? In light of the vision, is that where you want to go and is that what you want to become? and (2) Do you want to learn from me? This question goes beyond the person being a learner to credibility and trust factors that will allow mentoring to take place.

STRATEGY

We can build how we'll accomplish the vision around using what I call a "balanced spiritual diet." When asked to identify the basic food groups, most young people reply with McDonald's, Burger King, Pizza Hut, and Taco Bell. However, nutritionists know better. Currently, we're told that a healthy diet consists of six basic food groups. Each food group provides some but not all of what is needed. A healthy diet requires the right balance of all six.

Effective mentoring has four basic ingredients for a healthy spiritual diet. These four ingredients form the structure for our intentional time together, which can be either formal or very casual. The amount of each ingredient may vary but overall we need to strive for balance.

MENTORING—A BALANCED SPIRITUAL DIET

When I meet with those I'm mentoring, I plan my time around these four ingredients:

1. Progressive Relationship
2. Practical Truth
3. Pertinent Issues
4. Personal Questions

I don't have to put something in each group each time we meet. But over time, I want to ensure that a balanced diet is achieved. Sometimes I come prepared to cover a Practical Truth and find that the Spirit of God is focusing on a Pertinent Issue. Be sensitive to where God is working. Allow God's Spirit to lead you both in planning and in adjusting your plan. Let's look at each of these basic spiritual food groups individually.

1. PROGRESSIVE RELATIONSHIP

Remember the phrase "does anybody really know and does anybody really care"? People seem to be asking that. People aren't just spiritual—they're also social, intellectual, and physical. We're told in Luke 2:52 that Jesus grew in all four areas. We need to relate to the whole person. We should be asking how we can get to know a mentoree better considering all four areas of a person's life. This involves two-way communication, spending time together, doing activities together, and serving each other.

The word *consider* in Hebrews 10:24-25 means to give thought to, plan, or consider ahead of time. As disciplers, we need to intentionally connect with the other person in a comprehensive life setting. The greater the areas of contact, the more effective the impact.

Setting the right environment is a critical part of mentoring. The environment answers the question, "Is the relationship safe?" A greenhouse is a safe environment for plants. Protected and controlled, it allows the plants to get a healthy start. Mentoring should be a spiritual greenhouse for safe growth. New believers need an environment where they are:

- listened to
- taken seriously
- understood
- accepted

Each time I meet with someone I'm mentoring, I spend some initial time connecting relationally—getting caught up since our last meeting. Once we establish a deeper relationship, catching up is usually adequate. In the beginning, we may need to spend a larger proportion of time in this ingredient than we will later.

2. PRACTICAL TRUTHS

This ingredient deals with the "truths" of the Christian life. These truths are to be modeled, taught, and developed. This usually takes place in the form of some kind of Bible study. This time in Scripture may be casual or formal. It may come from a published Bible study or meditating over a passage of Scripture.

The Navigator's "Wheel" illustration is a good model for identifying some basic truth concepts and skills that young believers need to grow as disciples. These fundamentals are like the basic skills in baseball. No matter how advanced players are, they always need to practice the fundamentals.

This ingredient of spiritual mentoring is critical for authentic growth. Paul stresses this to Timothy in 2 Timothy 3:16-17: "All Scripture is God-breathed and is useful for teaching, rebuking, correcting and training in righteousness, so that the man of God may be thoroughly equipped for every good work."

3. PERTINENT ISSUES

This ingredient deals with real and current life issues. In real life in real time, issues seem to surface that we don't plan. Often they surface out of crises, need, or adversity. At other times, they surface from changes in circumstances or inviting opportunities.

As the mentoree shares concerns or as the mentor makes observations, they can identify these issues. I find that usually pertinent issues revolve around character. Sometimes I make a list of the pertinent issues I observe and let the mentoree make his own list. We then take turns addressing items on our lists. This way we both address what we feel is important.

Dealing with pertinent issues means looking at life issues through the lens of Scripture. What does Scripture say? Do beliefs, practices, or attitudes exist that aren't in alignment with God's life manual? Do some areas of life still need to be brought under the authority of the Word? The mentor and mentoree can usually identify these issues because a life area is broken and not working.

4. PERSONAL QUESTIONS

What does the mentoree want to know? This is a chance for him to ask anything he wants about becoming a mature follower of Christ. We often assume that because we've talked about a subject, the people we're mentoring get it—but they may not. We need to allow the opportunity for people to raise questions even if we don't have answers. These questions may require mentors to do some additional study and return to the issues later.

THE DIET IN PRACTICE

Sometimes when I meet with a person, I cover the four spiritual food groups in order. But other times I mix them up. We may be discussing a Practical Truth when we hit on a Pertinent Issue. The mentor needs wisdom and discernment to ensure that the diet stays balanced. Too much time on the relationship leaves the person starved for truth. Too much time on Practical Truth leaves the person starved for authentic relationship.

If I have an hour scheduled to spend in a mentoring setting, I usually plan on spending about 25 percent on the Progressive Relationship, 50 percent on the Practical Truth and the other 25 percent on either Pertinent Issues or Practical Questions.

The following chart can be a helpful tool for disciplers to use as they meet with a growing disciple. I refer to it as "Charting the Course." This planning guide helps you keep current, especially if you are meeting with more than one person. I fill this out before and after I meet with the growing disciple. I can use it to pray over during the week and as a way to check to see if the spiritual diet is balanced. You can copy this form or create your own using these ideas.

Charting the Course

Person _____ Date _____ Place _____

Prayer:	**Plan:**

Progress:

Possible Future Ideas:	**Prayer Items:**

Person, Date, and Place: Basic facts of the mentoring time

Prayer: These are areas and issues where I'm praying for the growing disciple. These may be issues that the disciple asks prayer for or issues I observe and have concerns about.

Plan: This is what I intend to cover as we meet. This agenda is set in agreement with the growing disciple as an upfront contract. This allows us to agree on expectations. When using the Balanced Spiritual Diet plan, this allows me to focus our meeting on the part of the diet that's essential right now.

Progress: These are notes I make for myself after our meeting to keep me focused on what's taking place. It might be answers to prayer, victories won, or temporary setbacks.

Possible Future Ideas: This is a place to record ideas for discussion or study. If the new idea stands the test of time and prayer, I then can address it in a future time with the growing disciple.

Prayer Items: The meeting time may generate new issues for prayer either directly or indirectly.

QUESTIONS FOR REFLECTION

1. From the definition of mentoring, why is it so vital?
2. How can a person be proactive in planning in the elements of a spiritual mentoring diet?

▶ TIPS FOR DISCIPLING

Guidelines and Checklist for the One-to-One Discipler
by Jack Griffin

1. Make sure you're well prepared. Pray before spending one-to-one time with someone, and organize yourself.
2. Remember that you can't lead anyone further than you have gone. You can't lay solid foundations in someone else's life with what are only sketchy outlines in your own.
3. Teach by the example of your life. The person who's ministering one-to-one must be what he's trying to teach.
4. Tailor your help to meet the needs of the individual. All people are different. Don't try to pour them all into the same mold.
5. Repeat everything. "He tells us everything over and over again, a line at a time and in such simple words!" (Isaiah 28:10, TLB). Don't apologize for repeating things.
6. In everything, show him how. We're generally too long in telling people what to do, and too short in showing them how.
7. Give achievable assignments. If you shovel everything you have at the disciple, throw away your shovel. Get out an eyedropper or a thimble.
8. Take nothing for granted. Check and double-check his progress on past commitments. "How have you been doing in your quiet times these last two weeks, Joe?"

9. Emphasize the lordship of Christ. Jesus said, "Anyone who does not carry his cross and follow me cannot be my disciple" and "Any of you who does not give up everything he has cannot be my disciple" (Luke 14:27 and Luke 14:33).

10. Help him establish his goals in life—the goals of knowing Christ and making him known.

11. Meet his needs through the Scriptures.

12. Keep sharing with him the importance of the "basics"—God's Word, prayer, fellowship, witnessing, and keeping Christ at the center of everything. "For no one can lay any foundation other than the one already laid, which is Jesus Christ" (1 Corinthians 3:11).

13. Explain the 2 Timothy 2:2 principle—concentrating on faithful men who will be able to teach others also. Teach him to give his life to a few, who in turn will multiply into many. Keep sharing the vision of disciplemaking (Matthew 28:19-20).

14. Remember Psalm 127:1—"Unless the Lord builds the house, its builders labor in vain." It is God who builds disciples. He is the Master Trainer.[4]

LAYING
THE
FOUNDATION

FOLLOW ME

LESSON PLAN

- Share highlights from personal devotional times.
- Review Matthew 4:19-20 and other verses memorized so far.
- Discuss the Bible study "Follow Me."
- Discuss the article "Questions I'd Ask Before Following Jesus."
- Share some stories about what has happened as a result of beginning to meet with people.
- Discuss Tips for Discipling: "Doing a Life-to-Life Session."

ASSIGNMENT FOR SESSION 6: PARENTAL PRAYER

- Prepare Bible study on "Parental Prayer."
- Read the article "The Prayers of a Leader."
- Memorize Philippians 1:3-4.
- Review daily the verses memorized.
- Continue personal devotional times.
- Identify nonChristians in your networks who you are praying for and relating to.
- Read Tips for Discipling: "Link Discipling and Outreach."

GROUP PRAYER REQUESTS

▶ BIBLE STUDY

FOLLOW ME

KEY ISSUES

- What did Jesus mean when He said, "Follow Me"?
- What did the first disciples learn about following Christ?
- What are the costs and benefits of following Christ today?

When Jesus came announcing the kingdom of God, He didn't tell people simply to say a prayer or follow a code of conduct. He said, "Come, follow me" (Matthew 4:19). The concept of following has lost much of its original meaning in our contemporary society. In sports, fans are "followers" of their favorite teams. They're informed, knowledgeable, and excited about being followers.

But is this what Jesus meant?

Jesus implied a lot more than being a fan when He challenged people to follow Him. What did it mean to those who became His first followers? What does it mean today? How does it affect a ministry of discipling others? We want to explore these questions in the study ahead.

Read the following paragraphs by David Hazard and underline what stands out to you.

"Follow Me," said Jesus.

So many of us hear Jesus' call today and set off after Him, eager as His first-century disciples were to possess the forgiveness and freedom from sin that He promised. It's easy to read the gospels and imagine ourselves right in among the people of Jesus' day, and to feel their enthusiasm as they responded to His call.

Peter hung up his nets and trailed after Jesus as He fished for souls during three years of teaching, healing, and performing miracles. Mary Magdalene left her bedeviled life. Andrew, and other disciples of John the Baptist, heard their new master repeat the word that generations of Jews had waited to hear: "The Kingdom of God is at hand!"

These followers recognized the beginning of the disciples' spiritual path. Eagerly they left behind the lives they knew and, literally, walked with Jesus. But where would the path of discipleship lead?

The will and work of God was about to be spread throughout towns, nations, and continents—and in order for this to occur, the will and work of God first spread its rule in their hearts. After all, where two wills are at work there is only a struggle for control.

"My Kingdom is a spiritual kingdom," Jesus told them. "My kingdom is within you."

So the question was this: Would they follow by imitating God and the Son of Man, humbly placing themselves—soul and being—under the governing direction of the Father? Would they turn away from their self-centered, self-directed ways to take part in higher purposes?

For quite a few disciples, that was too challenging. They slipped quietly away, turning back to their trades and families. Back home in the community they could still insist, "Yes, I believe in Jesus." And how would their closest friends know if, in the innermost places of their hearts—where life is governed by unseeable motives—they had refused to follow God's royal road to heaven?

Jesus' offer of forgiveness and eternal life is as attractive now as in the day when fishermen, soldiers, and outcasts first received it. Many of us jumped from our seats when we heard His call—"Follow Me"—through the appeals of contemporary evangelists. Others were prompted by the disgusting mess drugs, alcohol, or an unconscious libido had left on us. Like the first disciples, many of us have set out to be Christians.

But quickly we run into questions and confusion. Is it enough just to believe—or do I have to obey God? What is the evidence of the promised change in my life as a believer—is it a change in my doctrine only, and lifestyle choices, or is it transformation of my spirit and character? Where do my personal aspirations and dreams fit? How do I even begin, when every Christian I meet seems to have a different understanding of what it means to be a disciple?[1]

1a. In Matthew 6:33 Jesus said, "But seek first [Gods'] kingdom . . . " Why would *you* say it's important for a follower of Christ to have an understanding about the kingdom of God?

1b. What is important for a kingdom citizen to understand about "following"?

JESUS' INVITATION TO FOLLOW HIM

Fishing was a major industry around the Sea of Galilee. James and his brother, John, along with Peter and Andrew, were the first disciples Jesus called to work with Him. Jesus' call motivated these men to get up and leave their jobs—immediately. They didn't make excuses about why it wasn't a good time. They left at once and followed. Jesus calls each of us to follow Him. They weren't in a hypnotic trance when they followed, but were thoroughly convinced that following Him would change their lives forever. Jesus was calling them away from their productive trades to be productive spiritually. Jesus told Peter and Andrew to leave their fishing business and become "fishers of men," to help others find God.

In the first four chapters of his gospel, the apostle John recorded events that took place during the first year of Christ's ministry. Luke 5 and Matthew 4 record events sometime early in the second year of ministry. Read Matthew 4:18-22; Luke 5:1-11; and Luke 5:27-32; and answer the following questions:

2a. Why did these men leave what they were doing to follow Christ?

2b. How would their understanding of who Jesus was affect their willingness to follow?

2c. What were the implications of following Him for those first disciples?

2d. Remembering that they were being called away from something, does "follow me" normally suggest leaving something behind? If so, what might you need to leave behind?

PETER LEARNS THE MEANING OF "FOLLOW ME"

Peter was the most visible and outspoken disciple. We have snapshots of his journey, including his failures and successes.

3a. Read and meditate on the following passages to learn what Peter needed to understand about himself, Christ, and the kingdom in order to follow Christ.

Matthew 16:13-23; Luke 22:54-62; John 6:60,64-69; John 21:15-22

3b. Summarize what he needed to change in his thinking.

3c. How does the Holy Spirit help us with our willingness to follow Christ?

JESUS TEACHES ABOUT HELPING OTHERS FOLLOW

Jesus teaches not only about following Him but also about helping others follow Him. Jesus was constantly teaching about the meaning of following Him. He used a variety of opportunities to broaden the disciples' understanding.

4a. What do the following verses teach us about following Christ and helping others follow Christ?
John 13:12-17

John 13:34-35

4b. What does teaching the principle of following involve?

4c. Read the following passages and note the costs and benefits associated with following Jesus. Sometimes the concept of following is translated as "come after Me," or "come to Me."

Verses	Costs	Benefits
Matthew 10:34-42		
Matthew 11:28-30		
Mark 10:17-22,28-31		
Luke 9:23-26		
John 15:15-17		

4d. What ramifications do the passages have for following Christ in your own situation?

4e. Why did Christ emphasize both the costs and the benefits?

4f. Is "follow me" an invitation or a command? Why?

"FOLLOW ME"—THE CHALLENGE FOR TODAY

5a. What are the obstacles to following Christ today?

5b. What major lessons have you learned about following Christ during your spiritual journey?

5c. What costs and benefits have you experienced as you follow Christ?

SUMMARY

6. Write a summary or mission statement of what it means for you to follow Christ in the twenty-first century.

A PARABLE

At first I saw Christ as my observer, my judge, keeping track of the things I did wrong, so as to know whether I merited heaven or hell when I die. He was out there, sort of like the president, I recognized His picture when I saw it, but I really didn't know Him.

But later on, when I recognized His presence, it seemed as though life was rather like a bike ride, but it was a tandem bike, and I noticed that Christ was in the back helping me pedal.

I don't know just when it was that He suggested we change places, but life hasn't been the same since. When I had control, I knew the way. It was rather boring but predictable. It was the shortest distance between two points.

But when He took the lead, He knew delightful long cuts, up mountains and through rocky places and at breakneck speeds. It was all I could do to hang on! Even though it looked like madness, He said, "Pedal!"

I worried and was anxious and asked, "Where are You taking me?" He laughed and didn't answer, and I started to learn to trust.

I forgot my boring life and entered into the adventure. When I'd say, "I'm scared," He'd lean back and touch my hand.

He took me to people who had gifts I needed—gifts of healing, acceptance, and joy. They gave me their gifts to take on my journey, Christ's and mine.

And we were off again. He said, "Give the gifts away; they're extra baggage, too much weight." So I did, to the people we met, and I found that in giving I received, and still our burden was light.

I didn't trust Him at first, in control of my life. I thought He'd wreck it. But He knows bike secrets, knows how to make it bend to take sharp corners, jump to clear high rocks, fly to shorten scary passages.

And I'm learning to be quiet and pedal in the strangest places, and I'm beginning to enjoy the view and the cool breeze on my face with my delightful constant companion.

And when I'm sure I just can't do it any more, He just smiles and says, "Pedal."

AUTHOR. UNKNOWN

Questions I'd Ask Before Following Jesus

by Gordon MacDonald

I'M ROMANCED BY AIRPLANES. And part of the attraction has included the dream of possessing a pilot's license. A longtime fantasy: me, screaming down the runway (in a plane, of course) with one hand on the yoke and the other on the throttle. That fantasy is nearly fifty years old.

Flying lessons have always remained on life's waiting list for me. I had other, more pressing demands. College, or raising children, or book deadlines, or a church congregation.

Recently, a friend said, "I own a plane; I'll give you the basic instruction you'll need to get certified for your license." I thought I'd died and gone to heaven. Even my dear wife said, "Go for it; you've been talking about this all your life."

Suddenly there were no obstacles between me and my dream. So why did I hesitate? Why a sudden burst of uncertainty?

Questions suddenly arose: Was I really prepared to invest the necessary time? What other priorities would I need to downsize? How much technical reading (the kind I don't like) would be necessary? How much information to master—about navigation, radios, climate, aerodynamics, technologies, and mechanics? What if I failed? Or succeeded? How often could I fly? And could I (should I) really afford the costs of flying?

The original obstacles made it unnecessary to face these issues before. I'd never really discussed them with myself.

But here was the knockout punch. I imagined the day when a flight instructor would climb out of a plane and say to me, "Take her up by yourself. When (if?) you get back, I'll be here waiting for you." And I imagined myself up there—afraid to land. And it occurred to me that I loved the idea of flying more than I loved the reality.

Did I really want to break the bonds of earth? I heard myself say, "Nahhhh!" And instantly a dream died. The will to head for flight school just wasn't there. The questions had forced unanticipated conclusions. (Kudos to all pilots who are unafraid to land their planes.)

LOOKING BEFORE LEAPING

My reaction to a friend's kind invitation helped me appreciate what Simon Peter and friends faced on the Galilean beach when Jesus entered their world and invited them to another kind of flying—the building of the Kingdom of God.

I wonder what questions exploded in their minds when they heard the "follow Me" challenge? What issues concerned them? Practical questions? Personal questions? Priority questions? Questions about inadequacy? Anxiety? Compensation?

Let me suggest a few they might have asked. They're the ones I would ask of anyone who invited me on a spiritual journey of this magnitude. The cost of discipleship is enormous. We shouldn't take it on without an interrogation.

You see, eventually, each would-be disciple stands on something like the beach where Jesus approached Peter, James, and John with His challenge. On that beach we make a choice to follow the Lord and His designated discipler: to reshape life; to realize hidden, heaven-given potential; to become something of an influence; to align with God's purposes. What do we need to know before we leave our beach and move into motion? Here are some thoughts.

WHY DO YOU WANT ME, WITH ALL MY BAGGAGE?

As far as I know, none of the original disciples came to their beaches with anything of worth from their private pasts. Judas Iscariot may have looked the most promising! For the most part, the Lord's candidates for apostleship were simple, rural men. A few others had some sleaze in their résumés. The overall performances and attitudes of this group on several occasions reveal that their earlier character formation left something to be desired. This was no all-star team.

Simon Peter was raising the "baggage" issue when he said, "Go away from me, Lord; I am a sinful man" (Luke 5:8). Jesus' response: "Don't be afraid" (Luke 5:10).

It seems instructive that Jesus did little talking about His disciples' pasts. You would think we'd have heard a lot about Matthew's way of life as a tax collector or about Simon the Zealot's association with a political movement known for violence. But we don't. Jesus never exploits their "testimonies." If dark moments existed in the backgrounds of the Twelve (and there had to be), Jesus downplayed them, buried them in redemption. The Lord simply didn't deal with the pasts of people in public. And, thankfully, the gospel writers chose the same policy.

This has to encourage those of us with spiritual and moral résumés that are regrettable. We're tempted to believe that no future exists for us in the apostolic venture. Not so on the Galilean beach; not so now. Remember, Jesus took that first group and turned them into Kingdom champions. No one was beyond redemption, beyond the possibility of life change.

Now we do have to deal with baggage (as we're calling it); a call to discipleship involves renunciation. We need to resolve our baggage—not instantly, but in time through repentance and grace. There must be openness to new disciplines, new thinking, and new ways of relationship.

But the Lord always began right where people were. Shallow character, questionable reputation, and pessimistic perspectives were no deterrence to getting underway. All that was necessary was the willingness to lay that baggage at His feet. Without that willingness, a disciple is not a complete disciple.

WHAT MADE YOU INVITE ME?

In virtually every personal encounter with people, Jesus appears to have started with the bias of the heart rather than with an evaluation of outward performance. No small matter here. Jesus wasn't a talent scout; He was a student of the inner person. We tend to do our "headhunting" on the basis of achievement, social skills, education, and perceived potential. We give tests, compare vitae, and conduct interviews. Thankfully, the Lord looks inward and assesses spiritual authenticity.

We can assume that each of the Twelve began association with Christ as part of crowds who came to hear Him teach. They began as spectators. Perhaps each time they joined a crowd they moved a bit closer to the front and stuck around to ask questions—as seekers.

But there must have come a day when they engaged Him privately, their hearts mysteriously warmed by His words and demeanor. The Lord read their hearts like a book, and eventually came His invitation on the beach: "Why don't you follow Me, share My mission?" And when they left the beach with Him, they completed the move from spectators to seekers to followers. Jesus had read them correctly. Hearts aroused, they'd begun the process of loving Him.

What would such an awakening look like today? It might begin with an awareness of our own spiritual darkness and a corresponding desire for life change. It might continue as a magnetic attraction to Jesus as Lord, to His ways and words as the only sane way to believe and live.

Additionally, we might demonstrate spiritual curiosity by the way we begin to look at our world and its people, seeing the brokenness of life and sensing a growing desire to do something that calls people to God. Without such a heart, a disciple isn't a complete disciple.

WHAT'S THE MOST IMPORTANT ATTRIBUTE OF A DISCIPLE?

"I will make you . . ." was probably a common theme when teachers invited students into a follow-me relationship. It was the commitment of a master to a follower. But the commitment anticipated a disciple who thirsted for learning, for a reshaping of life. This assumes submission. Obedience wouldn't be too strong a word. The issue of trust comes into play, too: a disciple's confidence that the discipler knows the way and is worthy to be followed. Boil it all down, and you get teachability.

I like that word. It suggests a follower passionate for growth and usefulness. When a person is teachable, he or she doesn't waste energy with useless debate and resistance. The discipler need not tiptoe through the truth. He or she can offer insight, correction, rebuke, and opportunity with the assumption that the disciples will joyfully receive it.

I suspect there may be a scarcity of teachable people today. A culture that encourages thoughtless defiance chokes out teachability. Wannabe disciples who lack teachable spirits barely make it beyond the beach. Better that they would never say yes to the invitation until they've examined themselves on this one.

Incidentally, teachability doesn't imply a sort of despotic control by the discipler. The same Lord who asked for obedience washed His disciples' feet as a servant. That provides the balance some are concerned about.

But the fact remains: Without the trait of teachability, a disciple isn't a complete disciple.

WHERE IS DISCIPLESHIP LIKELY TO TAKE ME?

While His disciples tended to be glued to the past and the present, Jesus focused on the future. He saw every incident, conversation, and learning experience in light of future maturity. His rebuke, for example, which might sting for a day or two, wasn't meant to humiliate. Rather, it was designed to form character for harsh times ahead. His call to submission was directed at breeding leadership sensitivity. His two-by-two assignments to ministry were aimed at providing a clear picture of the Kingdom mission.

If you're Jesus and your disciples shove the children away because they're not significant, you keep in mind the day when they will preach to the crowds in lands and cultures they've never heard of. If you're Jesus and your disciples tell a man who's doing good to stop ("because he's not one of us"), you remind yourself that a time will come when they'll learn to rejoice at any evidence that God's hand is at work. If you're Jesus, you don't despair over today's incomplete picture; you concentrate on what's coming tomorrow. Always, on each occasion, the Lord was bringing the picture of their future into clearer focus. We can't gloss over this if we desire discipleship. The picture Jesus has of us puts personality, character, habits, and ambitions on the line. It says that Christlikeness is the issue and the goal. Jesus will make every effort to reshape us into godly people. This is a lifelong process, sometimes painful, sometimes humbling, sometimes tiring . . . but rewarding for the one who stays the course. A would-be disciple might want to ask: Do I trust His picture more than I trust the one I've formed for myself? The question isn't a shallow one. Without a hunger for Christlikeness, a disciple isn't a complete disciple.

WILL I BE ALONE IF I FOLLOW?

Absolutely not! Jesus wasn't in the business of developing solo performers. He was in the initial stages of building a church. And the church would provide an alternative to a dominant culture marked by cruelty and injustice, exploitation and greed, death and more death. He was establishing a new community; the original Twelve were the prototype.

So we're not talking disciple (singular); we're talking disciples (plural).

A community has a way of life, ethics and morals, disciplines, and goals. And a community, whether it realizes it or not, has something of a covenant: how it will pursue harmonious relationships and encourage the best from one another. Jesus began building this into His disciples from the get-go. Rugged individualism wouldn't work here. These men were never sent to do anything alone. They learned to work in pairs, in teams, in groups. Jesus modeled and encouraged interdependence; mercy and grace in times of failure and conflict were the order of the day. By the time the Master was through with them, these twelve individuals were a community, ready to offer leadership in the shaping of a considerably larger community. Their performance in Acts proves it.

A modern disciple must ask: "Am I prepared to get along with folks who are considerably different from me? Am I ready to master the graces of appreciation, encouragement, rebuke, and correction? Will I be open to learning how to forgive, how to repent, how to submit? Am I willing to be second banana today and first banana tomorrow?" It may be that we aren't prepared for discipleship if we're not prepared to learn the lessons and disciplines of community.

There are no solo disciples in the life of the Lord. So why do we try to produce such today? It doesn't work. Genuine discipleship in part is certified by the way a man or woman knows how to connect with brothers and sisters. Only then does the world "know that you are [Christ's] disciples" (John 13:35).

Without such a community, a disciple just isn't a complete disciple.

WILL YOU REJECT ME WHEN I FALL FLAT ON MY FACE?

An overview of how many times the original disciples fell short of reasonable expectations will quickly remind any would-be disciple that the process of apostolic development includes disappointment. Failure was all over the menu of the original Twelve, but rejection wasn't.

If Jesus ever grew discouraged over the Twelve, we don't hear about it. It sounds as if there was some occasional anger but not impatience; some stern warnings, but never threats. You soon realize that Jesus knew the hearts of these men better than they knew themselves. He recognized what we often don't: that the way to Christian maturity is paved with a thousand errors. We tend to write off one another and continue on our self-righteous way. Not our Lord. He never gave up.

It might be smart to take this self-examination: Am I prepared to be stretched to the point of inadequacy? To play with pain? To seem the fool? To get in over my head? Because these are all likely, and they can mean defeat. But from such experiences come champions of the kingdom variety. Tough, conditioned, wise champions.

Without learning humility through failure and errors, a disciple isn't really a complete disciple.

WHERE WILL I FIND THE POWER TO BE AND DO WHAT YOU ASK OF ME?

Of all the things Jesus did in the company of the Twelve, this seems the most incredible: He took a ragtag group of men who showed relatively little promise and delegated to them the mission of world evangelization.

For the most part the disciples seem to have felt secure and empowered as long as Jesus was with them. Of course, we see them scrambling to the back of the boat in the midst of a storm they were supposed to handle (at least some of them). "Do something!" is their cry to the Lord.

We see them wringing their hands because they're unable to rebuke a demon in the life of a small boy. Again: "Do something!"

But at the other end of the discipleship journey, Jesus would say, "You do something!" (such as disciple the nations!).

With that challenge (and this is the answer to the question) comes the promise of the energy of His Spirit. Ancient men understood a promise like this while we struggle with this notion that one could entrust his spirit to another. In this case the spirit is the Holy Spirit, and if this Spirit were upon the disciples (a storm-stilling, demon-rebuking, life-changing Spirit), then preaching to crowds on Pentecost, healing the sick, bringing the church to the nations wouldn't be impossible.

Would-be disciples of modern times need to be reminded that education, talent, and charisma have relatively little value in the Kingdom. These qualities are indeed helpful to possess, but without the inner dynamic energy of the Spirit of Jesus, they're useless when it comes to doing work with an eternal purpose.

Without the inner work of the Holy Spirit, a disciple isn't a complete disciple.

WHAT ARE THE RISKS OF FOLLOWING YOU?

Jesus didn't tell the Twelve everything at once. He unfolded the deeper teaching on Christlike growth, the implications of a worldwide mission, and ultimate martyrdom in direct proportion to the maturity of the disciples. He put no greater burden on them than they could bear. If He'd told them everything right at the start, my sense is that most of them would have bailed out. So it took some time to go from "Follow Me" to "When you are old you will stretch out your hands, and someone else will dress you and lead you where you do not want to go" (John 21:18). Better that words like these wait until a person has done some growing up at the soul level.

But the answer to the question always existed for those who wanted to face it: How risky? You'll die for Me. It sounds like disciples are dying in Christ's name almost every day around the world. It just isn't happening that much in North America. But it could and just might one day. If you enlarge "dying" to include careers lost, high incomes forfeited, friends lost, and security seemingly uncertain, then maybe the dying has started here already.

Of this we can be sure: Apart from the willingness to follow Him into death, a disciple isn't a complete disciple.

REALITY CHECK

It's too easy to glamorize discipleship—like I glamorized flying until someone challenged me to force my fantasy through the filter of reality. So also the follow-me invitation. Call what I've written the beach questions. The experiences I've had convince me that the answers to those questions are good ones. No regrets about not flying; and no regrets when Christ and those who discipled me invited me to follow.[2]

---◆---

ABOUT THE AUTHOR: Gordon MacDonald is senior minister at Grace Chapel in Lexington, Massachusetts. He's author of several books, including *Ordering Your Private World, When Men Think Private Thoughts, The Life God Blesses,* and *Christ Followers in the Real World* (all Thomas Nelson). On his days off, Gordon likes to walk in the woods with his wife, Gail. His favorite role these days is that of grandfather to five grandchildren.

QUESTIONS FOR REFLECTION

1. Which of the questions in this article do you most closely identify with? Why?
2. What unique questions would you ask before following Jesus at this new stage of becoming a discipler?

► TIPS FOR DISCIPLING

Doing a Life-to-Life Session
by John D. Purvis

Meeting life-to-life was a new experience for Jake. He was a new believer but a little skeptical about meeting with me. He wanted to grow in his faith but was suspicious about my suggestion that we get together for breakfast to discuss what growing in Christ is all about. After a couple of sessions, his fear evaporated and we enjoyed many hours together. His caution helped me to review the core elements of a life-to-life ministry that had helped me in discipling others for more than thirty years.

PREPARING

I spend five minutes praying for the person daily. This is the hardest yet most profitable preparation. Then once a week, when I have more time, I spend some extended time to intercede for him or her.

I like to formulate in advance the Bible part of our time together around a relevant spiritual truth using the acrostic PEAR. A Bible concordance can be a help.

> P—What's the relevant Scriptural *principle* (using a passage or key verses)?
> E—What *example* can I give from my life and/or from the life of a biblical character?
> A—What *application* can I suggest?
> R—Do I know of a *resource*—a book, tape, pamphlet, or website I can suggest?

BEGINNING

Most people need several minutes to download some of the routine arenas of their lives. This is a good time for me to practice listening skills of eye contact and feeding back questions to show that I understand. I ask with legitimate concern about the pressures or issues in their life. I try not to let this warm-up time take up the majority of our life-to-life time.

In my Day-Timer, I keep some questions to ask those I meet with. I keep notes of their answers. Because our goal is to see the character of Christ developed in each of our lives, I ask seven life-to-life, probing questions. I try to cover two of them each meeting:

1. What things went well this week?
2. What things went really horribly this week?
3. What caused you to really connect with God this week?
4. What made you back away from Him?
5. What one thing did you learn from your biggest mistake this week?
6. What's the most important thing you learned from Scripture this week?
7. What do you need me to pray for you after this meeting?

DURING

I allow adequate time to discuss the PEAR study I've prepared. One of the passages I gave Jake was from Luke 15. Because he was going through an excruciatingly painful family situation, I asked him to look at the passage not as a typical "prodigal son" but rather look for principles that characterized the loving actions of the father.

I then shared with him how a few years ago I caught a new glimpse of God's faithfulness as I was going through a difficult job change. We then turned to Psalm 34 where we looked at King David's reflection on the faithfulness of God.

For the application, I suggested that each morning during the following week Jake read through the Psalm we'd just discussed.

CONCLUDING

Realizing this life-to-life time together is a wartime event in the unseen spiritual realm, I always take time to pray together. If we're in a restaurant, which often we are, we simply leave our eyes open and talk to God conversationally. If it's convenient to go to the car, I find fewer distractions there. I tend to use Bible passages when I pray, to reinforce dependence on the Word of God. Over time, the person learns it's possible to accomplish serious kingdom business even in public.

After our meeting, I take time as soon as possible to review notes I took and to make additional observations.

PARENTAL PRAYER

LESSON PLAN

- Share highlights from personal devotional life.
- Review Philippians 1:3-4 and other verses memorized so far.
- Discuss "Parental Prayer" Bible study.
- Discuss "The Prayers of a Leader."
- Spend some time in prayer for those being discipled, using concepts from this session.
- Share the names of nonChristians each member is relating to and praying for.
- Use the "Who's on Your Heart for Heaven?" worksheet (page 218) to record names.
- Discuss Tips for Discipling: "Link Discipling and Outreach."

ASSIGNMENT FOR SESSION 7: FAITH AND THE PROMISES OF GOD

- Prepare the Bible study "Faith and the Promises of God."
- Read the article "Living by Promises."
- Memorize 2 Peter 1:4.
- Review past verses daily.
- Continue personal devotional times.
- Meet with your growing disciples.
- Read Tips for Discipling: "Promises to Claim for a Disciple."

GROUP PRAYER REQUESTS

▶ BIBLE STUDY

PARENTAL PRAYER

KEY ISSUES

- What is effective prayer?
- How can we be praying for our disciples?
- What's the core content of discipling prayer?

Any work of disciplemaking we do is only as effective as the touch of God: "Unless the LORD builds the house, its builders labor in vain" (Psalm 127:1).

Praying for those we're discipling is part of the work. Prayer activates the power of God and allows us to partner with His Spirit. We don't have to understand how prayer works to use it. We're told to pray and we have models of prayer. We must conclude that prayer isn't an option for the discipler.

E. M. Bounds declared that in the school of prayer, we're all in kindergarten. We have much to learn and apply. Whether we're coaches, new disciplers, or growing disciples, we are fellow strugglers.

A story has been told of J. O. Frazier, missionary to China, concerning the importance of prayer in helping believers grow in the Lord. He was helping two groups of Lisu tribal people simultaneously; one lived a distance away from Frazier and the other close by. He prayed more for the distant group because he wasn't able to be with them to give personal help and encouragement. Yet, on a later visit with that group, he discovered they were further along in their spiritual growth than the believers close by. It was a graphic illustration of the priority of prayer.

Prayer and the promises of God formed the foundation of The Navigators ministry. Dawson Trotman spent deep times with God in the Word and prayer—nights, days, weeks. Warren Myers once asked Lila, Dawson's widow, if Daws ever had a prayer conference. She said, "No, not exactly—but he had one-week prayer conferences with just two people: him and Jesus."

If you can only teach a disciple one thing, teach him or her how to pray. Your example of depending on God through prayer will encourage him or her to do the same. Start with praise and thanksgiving (see Hebrews 13:15). Many passages prompt praise and worship. Psalms 145–150 are filled with expressions of praise. Read a verse or two and then pray it back to God, adding any personal thoughts of your own. Start with sentence prayers.

But what do we pray for? Much of our prayer fits under the category of comfort. We want to relieve as much stress as we can and to make the person comfortable. But if you're a parent, you know that there are more important things than comfort. This is true for spiritual children as well. Certainly, prayer for the prevention and removal of pain and discomfort is worthy of our prayer efforts. But we can observe some key areas of prayer from Scripture that reflect the insight of a parent and we can know we are praying the will of God.

> This is the confidence we have in approaching God: that if we ask anything accord-
> ing to his will, he hears us. And if we know that he hears us—whatever we ask—we
> know that we have what we asked of him. (1 John 5:14-15)

Nothing can empower praying with confidence like knowing that we're asking for exactly what's on the heart of God—knowing that we are standing at the center of God's will. The Scriptures give us some help in knowing what to pray for as we're discipling others. God records some prayers of Jesus and Paul as they discipled others. From these models, we can learn not only to pray but what to pray for.

Take a look at what these parents/disciplers prayed, and allow it to focus your prayer for those you're discipling. These prayers demonstrate that what we pray for is of ultimate importance and that God uses prayer to bring about His plan. No matter how good a teacher or discipler or mentor you are, maturity requires the touch of God.

From these verses, you will summarize each prayer by listing in your own words what the parent/discipler was thankful and praying for. As you note the points of thanksgiving, you learn the importance of what was present in these new believers. As you're praying for your disciple, if these qualities aren't present for thanksgiving, make them a matter of prayer.

1. Meditate on the following prayers on page 106 and record your observations in the chart.

Sample: Ephesians 1:15-19 (MSG):

*That's why, when I heard of the solid trust you have in the Master Jesus and your out-
pouring of love to all the Christians, I couldn't stop thanking God for you—every time I
prayed, I'd think of you and give thanks. But I do more than thank. I ask—ask the God
of our Master, Jesus Christ, the God of glory—to make you intelligent and discerning in
knowing him personally, your eyes focused and clear, so that you can see exactly what
it is he is calling you to do, grasp the immensity of this glorious way of life he has for*

Christians, oh, the utter extravagance of his work in us who trust him—endless energy, boundless strength!

Paul was thankful for:

- *Their faith*
- *Their practical acts of love to others*

Paul prayed:

- *To know Jesus firsthand, personally*
- *For Wisdom and discernment*
- *For clear understanding*
- *To know what God is calling them to do*
- *To grasp His way of living*
- *To recognize His power at work in them*

Scripture	Thankful for	Prayed for	Desired results
1 Thessalonians 1:2-3			
1 Thessalonians 3:7-10			
2 Thessalonians 1:3-4			
2 Thessalonians 1:11-12			

Jesus is our model. He often spent whole nights in prayer. Prayer was the one thing the disciples asked Him to teach them.

2. John 17:6-26 is the recorded prayer of Jesus for His disciples. Study this prayer with the same observations as in question 1.

Scripture	Thankful for	Prayed for	Desired results
John 17:6-26			

Summarize your most significant observations:

JOY

The apostle John said, "I have no greater joy than to hear that my children are walking in the truth" (3 John 4). And the apostle Paul said, "You are our glory and joy" (1 Thessalonians 2:20). A search for the word *joy* in the epistles of John and Paul reveals a surprising pattern. In nearly every reference, the apostles' joy sprang directly from a discipling relationship. Even though Paul suffered greatly on these young believers' behalf, he counted the joy of seeing them grow well worth the cost (see Philippians 2:17; Colossians 1:24).

3a. What aspects of these relationships brought joy?

Romans 16:19

2 Corinthians 7:7

1 Thessalonians 2:19-20

2 Timothy 1:4

Philemon 7

2 John 1:4

2 John 1:12

3b. What rewards have you received from helping others grow? (If you haven't yet helped someone else to begin his or her journey of growth, interview an older Christian and ask how discipling has led to joy.)

3c. Does anything else in your life match the joy of seeing someone you're helping learn more about Jesus and become more like Him?

4. Paul asked for the prayers of others. From the following verses, what can you learn about praying for others?
Romans 15:30-31

Ephesians 6:18-20

Colossians 4:2-4

2 Thessalonians 3:1-2

SUMMARY

Urgency, priority, and expectancy all happen with prayer. Moreover, there's a recognized dependence on God to do what we can't. In the Greek language, a term is often connected with prayer that in the English language means to have an addiction. The word is translated as *constantly, devoted, earnestly, faithful,* and *devoted*. Paul wrote, "Epaphras, who is one of you and a servant of Christ Jesus, sends greetings. He is always wrestling in prayer for you, that you may stand firm in all the will of God, mature and fully assured" (Colossians 4:12). Let's be like Epaphras, who seemed to have a special awareness of the importance of prayer.

5. What changes do you need to make as you pray for your growing disciple?

The Prayers of a Leader

by J. Oswald Sanders

IN NOTHING SHOULD THE leader be ahead of his followers more than in the realm of prayer. Yet the most advanced Christian is conscious of the possibility of endless development in his prayer life. Nor does he ever feel he has "already attained." Dean C. J. Vaughan once said: "If I wished to humble anyone, I should question him about his prayers. I know nothing to compare with this topic for its sorrowful self-confessions."

Prayer is the most ancient, most universal, most intense expression of the religious instinct. It touches infinite extremes, for it is at once the simplest form of speech that infant lips can try and the sublime strains that reach the Majesty on high. It is indeed the Christian's vital breath and native air.

However, like a strange paradox, most of us are plagued with a subtle aversion to praying. We do not naturally delight in drawing near to God. We pay lip service to the delight and potency and value of prayer. We assert that it is an indispensable adjunct of mature spiritual life. We know that it is constantly enjoined and exemplified in the Scriptures. But in spite of all this, too often we fail to pray.

Let us take encouragement from the lives of men of like passions with ourselves who have conquered their natural reluctance and become mighty men of prayer.

The biographer of Samuel Chadwick wrote:

He was essentially a man of prayer. Every morning he would be astir shortly after six o'clock, and he kept a little room which was his private sanctum for his quiet hour before breakfast. He was mighty in public prayer because he was constant in private devotion. . . . When he prayed he expected God to do something. "I wish I had prayed more," he wrote toward the end of his life, "even if I had worked less; and from the bottom of my heart I wish I had prayed better."

"When I go to prayer," confessed an eminent Christian, "I find my heart so loath to go to God, and when it is with Him, so loath to stay." It is just at this point that self-discipline must be exercised. "When thou feelest most indisposed to pray, yield not to it," he counseled, "but strive and endeavor to pray, even when thou thinkest thou canst not pray."

Mastering the art of prayer, like any other art, will take time, and the amount of time we allocate to it will be the true measure of our conception of its importance. To most, crowding duties are a reason for curtailing time spent in prayer. To busy Martin Luther, extra work was a compelling argument for spending more time in prayer. Hear his answer to an inquiry about his plans for the next day's work: "Work, work from early till late. In fact I have so much to do that I shall spend the first three hours in prayer." If our view of the importance of prayer in any degree approximates that of Luther and Luther's Lord, we will somehow make more time for it.

It is of course true that prayer poses intellectual problems. But those who are skeptical of its validity and efficacy are usually those who do not seriously put it to the test, or who fail to comply with the revealed conditions. There is no way to learn to pray except by praying. No reasoned philosophy by itself ever taught a soul to pray. But to the man who fulfills the conditions, the problems are met in the indisputable fact of answered prayer and the joy of conscious fellowship with God.

For the supreme example of a life of prayer, the leader will naturally turn to the life of the Lord Himself, since belief in the rationality and necessity of prayer is based not merely on logic but preeminently on His example and precept. If prayer could have been dispensed with in any life, surely it would have been that of the sinless Son of Man. If prayer was unnecessary or unreasonable, we would naturally expect it to be omitted from His life and teaching. On the contrary, it was the dominant feature of His life and a recurrent element in His teaching. An examination of its incidence reveals that prayer kept the vision of His moral duty sharp and clear. It was prayer that nerved Him to do and endure the perfect but costly will of His Father. Prayer paved the way for the Transfiguration. To Him, prayer wasn't a reluctant addendum, but a joyous necessity.

Both our Lord and His bondslave Paul made it clear that true prayer is not pleasant dreamy reverie. "All vital praying makes a drain on a man's vitality. True intercession is a sacrifice, a bleeding sacrifice," wrote J. H. Jowett. Jesus performed many mighty works without outward sign of strain, but of His praying it is recorded that "he offered up prayers and supplications with strong crying and tears" (Hebrews 5:7, KJV).

How pale a reflection of Paul's and Epaphras's strivings and wrestlings are our pallid and languid intercessions! "Epaphras . . . is always wrestling for you in his prayers," wrote Paul to the believers at Colossae (Colossians 4:12, MLB). And to the same group, "I would that ye knew what great conflict I have for you" (Colossians 2:1, KJV). The word for wrestling, conflict, is that from which our *agonize* is derived. It is used of a man toiling at his work until utterly weary (Colossians 1:29); or competing in the arena for the coveted prize (1 Corinthians 9:25). It describes the soldier battling for his life (1 Timothy 6:12); or a man struggling to deliver his friend from danger (John 18:36). From these and other considerations, it is clear that true praying is a strenuous spiritual exercise that demands the utmost mental discipline and concentration.

THE HOLY SPIRIT KEY TO PRAYER

It is encouraging to recall that Paul, probably the greatest human exponent and example of the exercise of prayer, confessed, "We do not even know how we ought to pray." But he hastened to add, "The Spirit comes to the aid of our weakness . . . but through our inarticulate groans the Spirit himself is pleading for us, and God who searches our inmost being knows what the Spirit means, because he pleads for God's people in God's own way" (Romans 8:26-28, NEB). The Spirit links Himself with us in our praying and pours His supplications into our own.

We may master the technique of prayer and understand its philosophy; we may have unlimited confidence in the veracity and validity of the promises concerning prayer. We may plead them earnestly. But if we ignore the part played by the Holy Spirit, we have failed to use the master key.

Progressive teaching in the art of praying is needed, and the Holy Spirit is the master Teacher. His assistance in prayer is more frequently mentioned in Scripture than any of His other offices. All true praying stems from His activity in the soul. Both Paul and Jude teach that effective prayer is "praying in the Spirit." The phrase has been interpreted as praying along the same lines, about the same things, in the same name, as the Holy Spirit. True prayer rises in the spirit of the Christian from the Spirit who indwells him.

"Praying in the Spirit" may have a dual significance. It may mean praying in the realm of the Spirit, for the Holy Spirit is the sphere and atmosphere of the Christian's life. But in fact, many of our prayers are psychical rather than spiritual. They move in the realm of the mind alone, the product of our own thinking and not of the Spirit's teaching. But this is something deeper. The type of praying envisaged in this phrase "utilizes the body, demands the cooperation of the mind, but moves in the supernatural realm of the Spirit." This kind of prayer transacts its business in the heavenly realm.

But the phrase "praying in the Spirit" may also mean praying in the power and energy of the Spirit. "Give yourselves wholly to prayer and entreaty; pray on every occasion in the power of the Spirit," is the New English Bible rendering of Ephesians 6:18. For its superhuman task, prayer demands more than mere human power, and this is supplied by the Holy Spirit. He is the Spirit of power as well as the Spirit of prayer. Human energy of heart and mind and will can achieve only human results, but praying in the Holy Spirit releases supernatural resources.

THE SPIRIT AS ALLY

It is the Spirit's delight to aid the man entrusted with spiritual leadership in his moral and physical weakness in this matter of prayer, for the praying soul labors under three handicaps. But in each of them he may count upon the Spirit's assistance. Sometimes he is kept from prayer by the conscious iniquity of his heart. As he trusts Him, the Holy Spirit will lead him to and enable him to appropriate the cleansing of that mighty solvent, the blood of Christ. Then the spiritual leader is hampered by the ignorance of his mind. The Spirit who knows the mind of God will share that knowledge with him as he receptively waits on Him. He does this by imparting a clear conviction that a petition is or is not according to the will of God. Again, the spiritual leader will often be earthbound through the benumbing infirmity of his body. The Spirit will quicken his mortal body in response to his faith, and will enable him to rise above adverse physical conditions.

In addition to these personal handicaps, the praying man has to overcome the subtle opposition of Satan who will seek to oppress or depress, to create doubt or discouragement. In the Holy Spirit the praying man has been given a heavenly ally against a supernatural adversary.

DISARMING THE ADVERSARY

The foregoing thoughts are doubtless not new to many who have read them, but is the mighty assistance, the power, of the Spirit in prayer a present and enjoyed experience? Have we slipped into an unintentional independence of the Spirit in prayer? Are we habitually "praying in the Spirit" and receiving the full answer to our prayers? It is very easy for our intellectual apprehension of spiritual truths to outrun our practical experience of their reality and power.

Prayer is frequently represented in Scripture under the figure of spiritual warfare. "We wrestle . . . against principalities, against powers, against the rulers of the darkness of this world, against spiritual wickedness in high places" (Ephesians 6:12, KJV). In this phase of the prayer life, three personalities are involved, not two. Between God on the one hand and the Devil on the other, stands the praying man. Though weak in himself, he occupies a strategic role in the deathless struggle between the dragon and the Lamb. The power and authority he wields are not inherent but are delegated to him by the victorious Christ to whom he is united by faith. His faith is the reticulating system through which the victory gained on Calvary over Satan and his hosts reaches the captives and delivers them.

Throughout the gospels, the thoughtful reader will discern that Jesus was concerned not so much with the wicked men and the evil conditions He confronted as with the forces of evil at the back of them. Behind well-meaning and ever-vocal Peter, behind the traitorous Judas, Jesus saw the black hand of Satan. "Get thee behind me Satan," was the Lord's response to Peter's well intentioned but presumptuous rebuke. We see men around us bound in sin, and in captivity of the Devil, but our concern in prayer should be not only to pray for them but to pray against Satan who holds them captive. He must be compelled to relax his grip on them and this can be achieved only by Christ's victory on the Cross. Jesus dealt with the cause rather than the effect, and the leader should adopt the same method in this aspect of his praying. And he must know how to lead those under him to victory in this spiritual warfare.

In a graphic illustration, Jesus likened Satan to a strong man, fully armed, who kept his palace and goods in peace. Before he could be dispossessed and his captives released, Jesus said he must first be bound, or rendered powerless. Only then could the rescue be effected (Matthew 12:28-29). What does it mean to "bind the strong man," if not to neutralize his power by drawing on the conquering power of Christ who was manifested "to destroy [nullify, render inoperative] the works of the devil"? And how can this be done but by the prayer of faith which lays hold on the victory of Calvary and believes for its repetition in the specific context of the prayer? We must not make the mistake of reversing our Lord's order, and expect to effect the rescue without first disarming the adversary. The divinely delegated authority placed in our hands may be confidently exercised, for did not our Lord say to His weak disciples, "Behold, I have given you authority . . . over all the power of the enemy" (Luke 10:19, RSV)?

MOVING PEOPLE THROUGH PRAYER

Since leadership is the ability to move and influence people, the spiritual leader will be alert to discover the most effective way of doing this. One of the most frequently quoted of Hudson Taylor's statements is his expression of conviction that "it is possible to move men, through God, by prayer alone." In the course of his missionary career he demonstrated its truth a thousand times. However, it is one thing to give mental assent to his motto, but quite another thing consistently to put it into practice. Men are difficult objects to move, and it is much easier to pray for temporal needs than for situations that involve the intricacies and stubbornness of the human heart. But it is in just such situations that the leader must prove his power to move human hearts in the direction in which he believes the will of God lies.

In prayer, we deal directly with God, and only in a secondary sense with men and women. The goal of prayer is the ear of God. Prayer influences men by influencing God to influence them. It is not the prayer that moves men, but the God to whom we pray.

Prayer moves the arm

That moves the world

To bring deliverance down.

To move men, the leader must be able to move God, for He has made it clear that He moves them through the prayers of the intercessor. If a scheming Jacob could be given "power with God and with men," then is it not possible for any leader who is willing to comply with the conditions to enjoy the same power (Genesis 32:8)?

Prevailing prayer of this kind is the outcome of a correct relationship with God. Reasons for unanswered prayer are stated with great clarity in Scripture, and they all center around the believer's relationship with God. He will not be party to petitions of mere self-interest, nor will He countenance impurity of motive. Sin clung to and cherished will effectively close His ear. Least of all will He tolerate unbelief, the mother of sins. "He that cometh to God must believe."

Everywhere in prayer there is the condition, either expressed or implied, that the paramount motive in praying is the glory of God.

The eminence of great leaders of the Bible is attributable to the fact that they were great in their praying. They were not leaders because of brilliancy of thought, because they were exhaustless in resources, because of their magnificent culture or native endowment, but because by the power of prayer, they could command the power of God.[1]

———————◆———————

ABOUT THE AUTHOR: The late Dr. J. Oswald Sanders served as director of Overseas Missionary Fellowship and had a worldwide teaching ministry. He was the author of more than thirty books.

QUESTIONS FOR REFLECTION

1. Sanders states, "Most of us are plagued with a subtle aversion to praying. We do not naturally delight in drawing near to God." Why do you think this is true?

2. In view of the article, what's one upgrade in your prayer life where you believe God is prompting you? Is there anyone who could help encourage you?

▶ TIPS <u>FOR DISCIPLING</u>

Link Discipling and Outreach

by Alice Fryling

It's important for the person you're discipling to have a good start in witnessing within his or her sphere of influence to others. Here's how you can evaluate where you are in reaching out and helping someone else learn to witness:

1. Evaluate your feelings about sharing one's faith:

   - What thoughts and feelings do you have when you hear the words *sharing your faith*?
   - How was Christianity shared with you? What was positive for you? Negative?
   - What can you share about your nonChristian friends?
   - Which nonChristians are you actively praying for?
   - Which of them seem open to the gospel?
   - How do you feel about sharing your faith with that person?
   - What might be some first steps you could take?

2. Visit a Christian bookstore and determine a book on evangelism that might be suitable to read and discuss together, such as *Opening the Door* (NavPress), *Jesus Cares for Women* (NavPress), or *Out of the Saltshaker* (InterVarsity Press).

3. Study the Scriptures to gain a biblical basis of evangelism. Look at how Jesus related to people who He wanted to draw to Himself. Evaluate how these principles relate to your unique situation.

4. Pray regularly for your nonChristian friends.

5. If you or the person you are discipling has no nonChristian friends, consider how to build relationships outside of the "holy huddle." Begin to pray that God will bring nonChristians into your life. Participate in some activities that will allow you to meet new unchurched friends.

6. Seek out a mentor in evangelism. Invite yourself along when they're spending time with nonChristians.

7. Learn some easy-to-learn gospel presentations. Consider NavPress's "The Bridge to Life" or Campus Crusade for Christ's "Four Spiritual Laws." Roleplay the presentation with a friend or your new disciple, letting your friend present the gospel to you and respond to your questions and objections.[2]

FAITH AND THE PROMISES OF GOD

LESSON PLAN

- Share highlights from personal devotional lives.
- Review 2 Peter 1:4.
- Discuss "Faith and the Promises of God" Bible study.
- Discuss "Living by the Promises."
- Share from discipling ministry experiences.
- Pray for those you are discipling, using ideas from the studies "Parental Prayer" (pages 104-109) and "Description of a Disciple" (pages 54-61).
- Discuss Tips for Discipling: "Promises to Claim for a Disciple."

ASSIGNMENT FOR SESSION 8: HABITS OF THE HEART

- Prepare "Habits of the Heart" Bible study.
- Read articles on spiritual disciplines.
- Memorize 1 Timothy 4:7-8.
- Continue personal devotional times.
- Continue to meet with your growing disciple(s).
- Read Tips for Discipling: "Habits Make the Difference."

GROUP PRAYER REQUESTS

▶ BIBLE STUDY

FAITH AND THE PROMISES OF GOD

KEY ISSUES

- How do God's promises reflect His person and His purposes?
- What is God's pattern for claiming His promises?
- How do we base the ministry of discipling others on the promises of God?

Do we lurk in the premises or stand on the promises?

A SERMON TITLE, AUTHOR UNKNOWN

Promise: an oral or written agreement to do or not to do something; vow.

WEBSTER'S NEW WORLD DICTIONARY

We've all been affected by promises. We're promised things every day from all kinds of sources—from advertising to employers. Our experience with promises often leaves us skeptical when we get another one. Some promises are kept; others aren't.

The word *promise* in Scripture frequently signifies a gift graciously bestowed, not a pledge secured by negotiation. It's primarily a law term, denoting a summons or an undertaking to do or give something.

Following the promises of God should be the normal way of living for a follower of Christ. Discipling others creates an additional area of life and ministry where we need to capture the power of living by faith in the promises of God.

FOR REFLECTION

Describe an earlier experience when you took God at His word and believed a promise.

THE SIGNIFICANCE OF GOD'S PROMISES

Divine promise is a theme that runs throughout Scripture, and it is foundational to living and ministering in God's kingdom. From Genesis to Revelation, we're exposed to God's promises as He deals with people. The ultimate fulfillment of all God has promised is Christ Himself (see 2 Corinthians 1:20; Ephesians 3:6).

Some of the major promises of the Old Testament are:

- the promise to Adam and Eve that their seed would overcome Satan (Genesis 3:15)
- the promise to Noah that He would never again destroy the earth with a flood (Genesis 8:21-22; 9:1-17)
- the promise to Abraham to make of him a great nation in whom all families of the earth should be blessed (Genesis 12:2,7; Exodus 12:25; Deuteronomy 1:8,11; 6:3; 9:26-28)
- the promise to David to continue his house on the throne (2 Samuel 7:12-13; 1 Kings 2:24)
- the promise of restoration of Israel, of the Messiah, of the new and everlasting kingdom, of the new covenant and outpouring of the Spirit (Isaiah 2:2-5; 4:2; 55:5; 66:13; Jeremiah 31:31-34; 32:37-42; 33:14; Ezekiel 36:22-31; 37:11 and following; 39:25 and following)

1a. What are other major promises that stand out to you from Scripture?

Throughout history, as recorded in Scripture, God has consistently used promises along with commands to deal with His people. God uses promises (to guide, to reveal His will, and so on) for a variety of reasons.

1b. What do the following verses imply as the purpose behind His promises?
Deuteronomy 6:3

Romans 4:20-21

1 Corinthians 15:57-58

Hebrews 6:17

2 Peter 1:3-4

1c. What other reasons can you think of that shed light on why God uses promises? (Thinking about why we make promises may help get you started.)

Take the promises of God. Let a man feed for a month on the promises of God, and he will not talk about how poor he is. You hear people say, "Oh, my leanness! How lean I am." It is not their leanness, it is their laziness. If you would only read from Genesis to Revelation and see all the promises made by God to Abraham, to Isaac, to Jacob, to all the Jews and to the Gentiles, and to all His people everywhere—If you would spend a month feeding on the precious promises of God, you wouldn't be going about complaining how poor you are. You would lift up your head and proclaim the riches of His grace, because you couldn't help doing it!

D. L. MOODY

CLAIMING AND LIVING BY HIS PROMISES

Claiming or living by God's promises is simply a matter of identifying what He has promised to us and then by faith living in light of that promise. We find few formulas for living the Christian life in the Scriptures, but sometimes an outline can help us get hold of important concepts. Living by God's promises involves faith and obedience. The following are six questions that can help us understand, claim, and live by His promises.

1. Who made the promise?
2. What is the promise?
3. Who is the promise for?
4. What is to be believed?
5. What are the conditions?
6. What endurance is required?

WHO MADE THE PROMISE?
Behind the promises of God are His character and resources.

The principle of living by the promises of God is powerful because God's character guarantees it will happen. Our foundational Christian faith rests on what God has said—that He completes His commitments.

I (John) promised my young daughter that we would pay several thousand dollars toward her college expenses. Little did I know that medical, spiritual, and emotional difficulties would drain our account to almost zero. It seemed impossible for me to keep my word. The only option was a loan that I hadn't wanted to do. But because we had promised, we wanted to honor our promise the best way we could.

God not only desires to honor His promises, His resources are never in doubt. Our resources or ability may make it difficult—and in some cases impossible—to keep our promises. But God's ability and resources are limitless, making His promises sure.

Not one of all the LORD's good promises to the house of Israel failed; every one was fulfilled. (Joshua 21:45)

The Lord is not slow in keeping his promise, as some understand slowness. He is patient with you, not wanting anyone to perish, but everyone to come to repentance. (2 Peter 3:9)

A promise is no better than the character of the one making the promise. Before accepting or banking on a promise from people, we naturally ask, "How reliable is their word?"

2a. What do you observe from the following verses regarding God's Word and His character?
Numbers 23:19

1 Kings 8:56

Proverbs 30:5

Matthew 24:35

Romans 4:20-21

Hebrews 10:23

What Is the Promise?

Understanding what God has said in His promises is critical to living by them. Usually the context of the promise helps us know His meaning.

Who Is the Promise For?

Living by God's promises requires that we identify who the promise was given to. Some promises were given to specific individuals; others, to groups of people. Some are for a specific time and others for any time. However, much of what God promises is still intended for us today. If we fail to recognize these promises, we miss experiencing God's blessing and design.

2b. Look at the following passages and note what the promise was and who the recipients are.

Passage	What is promised?	Who are the recipients?
Acts 2:38-39		
Romans 4:16-17		
2 Corinthians 1:20-22		
Ephesians 3:6		
2 Peter 1:3-4		

What Is to Be Believed?

Every promise requires faith that ultimately is based on the character of God. Because a promise is about the future, faith is required. Sometimes the faith required touches more than the promise itself. As Hebrews 11:6 says, "Without faith it is impossible to please God, because anyone who comes to him must believe that he exists and that he rewards those who earnestly seek him."

What Are the Conditions?

There usually are qualifications to the promises, given in the form of "conditions" or "if clauses." Conditions don't contradict the gracious nature of the promise. Conditions don't imply any merit-oriented relationship with the promise; rather they identify those who qualify to receive the benefit of the promises.

The main condition regarding the promises of God is faith. Faith isn't a merit factor causing the promise to be given but rather a vehicle the promise is derived through. Conditions are to promises as planting and cultivating are to seeds. They don't cause the growth but they do make it possible.

2c. From the following passages, note the promise and the condition.

Passage	Promise	Condition
Proverbs 3:5-6		
Romans 8:28		
Genesis 12:1-3		
Joshua 1:8		
John 16:24		

2d. What other promises from God do you know that have conditions?

WHAT ENDURANCE IS REQUIRED?

God rarely gives and fulfills His promises at the same time. Waiting is part of God's pattern for living by promises: "You need to persevere so that when you have done the will of God, you will receive what he has promised" (Hebrews 10:36).

When we omit any of these five steps, we're in danger of missing God's design in giving us His promises.

Two young men, a world map between them, met forty-two days and prayed by an early morning campfire . . . Dawson Trotman, one of those men, had concluded that something which could or should be done was not being done, or the Great Commission would be nearer fulfillment. He put a finger on most of the countries of the world, asking God to raise up young people who would be used in making Christ known.

Eventually, certain promises from the Word came into focus. One was Isaiah 58:12 [KJV]: "Thou shalt raise up the foundations of many generations." Another was Isaiah 45:14 [KJV]: "Men of stature . . . shall come over unto thee." Daws was in awe of these promises—and though he realized that in context they were prophetic, he also knew that they were God's promises to him and he was staggered by their implications.

LORNE SANNY

The development and growth of The Navigators came about in fulfillment of specific promises of God involving the whole world.

CASE STUDIES

Two case studies from the Old Testament can give us insight in how to live by promises. Select at least one and make observations.

ISRAEL UNDER MOSES' LEADERSHIP

Read the summary in Deuteronomy 1:19-46 of the response that Israel made to God's promise of the Promised Land. (Remember that God had given and stated the promise through three generations: Abraham, Genesis 18:18-21; Isaac, Genesis 26:2-4; and Jacob, Genesis 35:11-12.)

3a. As you read Moses' review, look for answers to the following questions:
Why did they fail to receive what was promised?

What were *not* reasons for the failure?

What results did they experience?

How was it different under Joshua's leadership some forty years later?

DAVID AND GOD'S PROMISE OF A HOUSE

David desires to build a house for God. And in the process, God makes a promise to David.

3b. Read 1 Chronicles 17:1; 22:1; and 2 Chronicles 6:1-21; and answer the following questions.
What promise was given?

What did David believe?

What was his response?

What was the result?

3c. Contrast the life of a person who lives by faith in the promises of God with that of someone who doesn't. Imagine what each person would be like and describe him or her in the chart below.

Describe what life would be like if a person lived with his or her life based on faith in the promises of God.	Describe someone who *does not* live his or her life based on faith in the promises of God.

If some of the people you were counting on have decided they want to do other things this year, or if your income has been sagging, ask God to search your heart for any sin or wrong. Confess it, make it right—and then claim the promises of God . . . I met a great missionary who asked shortly after Daws died, "What promises from God are you claiming these days?" Without claiming the promises of God, The Navigators ministry never would have begun and without it, the work would wither and die.

May I remind you that promises from God, at least for me, do not come from casual flipping through the Bible, but rather they are born out of conflict and struggle. They are born out of much prayer and time in the Word.

Remember that you don't obey a promise; you believe it. God makes it happen, you don't. Because of His promises we obey His commands. We believe a promise, we obey a command.

LORNE SANNY

STRATEGIES THAT UNDERMINE LIVING BY GOD'S PROMISES

We all use devices or strategies, conscious and unconscious, for living out life. Some of these substitute for and hinder our dependence on God and keep us from building our lives on God's promises.

From a survey, here are some means others have stated they tend to fall back upon instead of depending on God and claiming His promises:

- making and executing our own plans
- past experience: "been there, done that"
- circumstances: "It happened this way with them. Why should it be different with me?"
- using our own logic or intellect: "Trust in the Lord sometimes, but lean *a lot* on my own understanding. I didn't pay eighty thousand dollars on an education for nothing; I'm going to use it."

Some boast in chariots, and some in horses;
But we will boast in the name of the LORD, our God. (Psalm 20:7, NASB)

4. What strategies do you tend to rely upon? What hinders you from walking by faith in the promises of God?

LIVING BY THE PROMISES OF GOD FOR MINISTRY

It's interesting to notice that ministry in the Scriptures often begins with a word or promise from God.

5a. As you reflect on some of the more familiar people in Scripture, what general observations do you make?

Abraham (Genesis 12:1-3)

Joshua (Joshua 1:1-9)

Gideon (Judges 6:11-16)

Hannah (1 Samuel 1:12-18)

Jeremiah (Jeremiah 1:1-10)

Mary, mother of Jesus (Luke 1:30-33)

As a student in college, I (Ron) began to get a heart and vision for discipling others. During my senior year, while attending a national collegiate conference in Colorado Springs, I heard a message on 1 Corinthians 15:58. It became a foundational promise that has given me encouragement for more than thirty years. When I'd get discouraged, lose focus, or not see much result, I'd review and pray over this promise.

5b. Why should you claim promises of God for your ministry of discipling others?

5c. What promises are you claiming by faith for your life and ministry?

5d. What implications does this study have on how you live and disciple others?

5e. What additional issues can you currently bring to God? Claim His promise.

Living by Promises

by Skip Gray

THE GREEK CONCEPT OF knowledge meant acquiring propositional truth—information gained and stored in the mind. However, the Hebrews saw knowledge as having to do with relationship and experience. The Old Testament says that Adam "knew" his wife (Genesis 4:1). To "know" her meant that he had an intimate husband-wife relationship with her.

The apostle Peter in the New Testament wrote in the Greek language, but he had a Hebrew mindset. He wrote, "His divine power has given us everything we need for life and godliness through our knowledge of him who called us by his own glory and goodness" (2 Peter 1:3).

He was saying that our intimate, personal, "marriage" relationship with Christ provides us with everything we need to live a godly life. So how do we enhance our marriage to Christ? How do we deepen our experience of Him? In the next verse, Peter wrote that God gave us "his very great and precious promises," so that through them we can participate in the divine nature and escape the corruption in the world caused by evil desires.

As we appropriate God's promises by faith, we enrich our communication with Christ, our trust and adoration of Him, and our obedience to Him. This is a lifetime process. The better we get to know Him—seeing Him make and keep promises—the greater confidence we'll have in His trustworthiness as the years go by. A beautiful marriage is a work of art that takes a lifetime to complete, and so does a beautiful Christian life.

A PROMISE FROM GOD IS A FACT

Another important passage which speaks of God's promises is 2 Corinthians 1:20. "For no matter how many promises God has made, they are 'Yes' in Christ." Therefore, through Him, we speak the "Amen" to the glory of God. God doesn't make any yes-and-no promises. All of His promises are positive, and in Christ, they are "So be it" and "Count it done." When God promises to do something, He will do it.

All this is for the glory of God. It's not so that any of us can be known as great promise-claimers. It's for God's glory, but it is "by us." You and I are the means, the vehicle, and the channel by which God glorifies Himself as we experience, appropriate, and claim the promises of God. We should claim these promises for ourselves, for our families, and for others we minister to.

GENERAL PROMISES

The Bible contains two kinds of promises: general promises, which apply to all Christians at all times under all circumstances; and specific promises, which apply only in certain situations. Examples of general promises are 1 John 5:11-12 ("God has given us eternal life, and this life is in his Son") and John 3:16 ("Whoever believes in him shall not perish, but have eternal life"). If you hear the gospel of Christ and believe it, you receive eternal life. This promise is always true. Whenever we're tempted to doubt it, we can go back to God's Word and ask, "What does God say?"

Another general promise is 1 John 1:9, which is the Christian's bar of soap: "If we confess our sins, he is faithful and just and will forgive us our sins and purify us from all unrighteousness." If you're a Christian, there will never be a time in your life when 1 John 1:9 isn't true for you and available when you need it. The Holy Spirit wants us to confess the sins He points out to us. When we're sensitive and responsive—confessing and making restitution if necessary—then God cleanses us from all unrighteousness. The slate is clean, and our channel of communication with the Father is wide open and perfect. Our intimacy with Him grows.

Incidentally, the difference between the conviction of the Holy Spirit and the accusation of Satan is threefold. When the Holy Spirit convicts of sin, the conviction is specific, gentle, and hopeful. However, the accusation of Satan is vague, harsh, and discouraging. If you're struggling with guilt, recognizing this difference can help you determine whether it's the Holy Spirit's work or the devil's.

Another general promise is Galatians 5:22-23: "The fruit of the Spirit is love, joy, peace, patience, kindness, goodness, faithfulness, gentleness and self-control." Have you ever met a Christian whose life didn't manifest all these qualities? Probably you have—perhaps while looking in the mirror this morning. However, why don't we experience all of them? Aren't they the fruit of the Spirit promised by God? Yes, but we may not experience these fruits because we aren't claiming this passage in prayer, and allowing the Holy Spirit to control us.

Claiming God's promises is the heart of our prayer life. We simply take back to God His promises of what He said He would do. We don't try to twist His arm and persuade Him to do something He's not inclined to do. We don't say, "Well, you probably don't want to do this for me, but I'd like to ask you anyway." No, God has said He will do it. It brings joy to the Father's heart when His children come to Him and say, "Please fulfill this promise in my experience today."

Another general promise is 1 Corinthians 10:13, which tells us that we have a way to escape temptation. We're all tempted, and when temptation comes we should ask, "Father, show me now the way of escape in this particular situation." The more specific we are with God in the way we claim His promises, the more specific He'll be with us. To pray, "Lord, bless _____ " may be only a salve for our conscience. That's all. Dawson Trotman used to mention the man whose prayer life consisted of glancing up at the framed copy of the Lord's Prayer on the wall each night before turning out the light, and saying, "Those are my sentiments"—click. No real substance. No real depth. Therefore, no deepening relationship with Christ.

The Bible contains an incredible wealth of promises from God that He wants us to appropriate and spend. So many Christians go through life "nickel-and-diming it." They have millions in the bank, but they won't write a check. They're afraid God will go bankrupt. They'd never admit that, but it's the way they live.

SPECIFIC PROMISES

God frequently gives guidance and direction to individual Christians in particular areas of life in a way that doesn't apply to the entire Body of Christ or to all the Christians in a given community. One illustration is found in Acts 13:47. The apostle Paul had preached the gospel to the Jews, but they'd rejected his message. Therefore, he said, he would turn to the Gentiles. "For this is what the Lord has commanded us: 'I have made you a light for the Gentiles, that you may bring salvation to the ends of the earth.'"

The passage Paul quoted was a messianic promise from Isaiah 49. This promise had been fulfilled in Jesus Christ. Now God led Paul in a new direction in his ministry through a secondary use of the promise. Every teaching of Scripture has one basic interpretation, but it can have several applications—and this is a case in point. The promise in Isaiah had one interpretation—Jesus Christ. It had one application in the coming of Christ, but it also had a secondary application (not an interpretation) in offering guidance for Paul as he shifted from ministering primarily to Jews to ministering to Gentiles. This verse didn't apply in this way to the entire body of Christ, but it did to Paul and his team.

STAYING SAFE

When we come to a promise of this kind, several guidelines can keep us from drifting off into error, imbalance, heresy, or some other harmful and subjective application.

First, many promises have the condition of our obedience to God.

Second, God will never lead you through one verse of Scripture to do something He clearly prohibits somewhere else in the Scriptures. We must be careful not to put a wrench on a passage in such a way that we say, "God led me to do this" about something God doesn't allow. Keep in mind the total witness of the Scriptures whenever you use a particular promise as the basis for making a decision.

Third, don't decide when and how a promise must be fulfilled. Don't prejudge God, or try to paint Him into a corner. Remember who is serving who. God isn't my servant; I'm His. He gives me the privilege of prayer and of claiming promises. But in doing that, He doesn't become my servant. God isn't my errand boy. I'm His servant and errand boy.

God wants us to know that He's loving, kind, wise, and gracious. He wants us to believe He's like this whether or not He answers our prayers the way we had in mind.

Fourth, present your need to God in prayer, and let God pick out the promise. Don't jump the gun. Don't be anxious. Don't turn the Bible into a magic book or a fetish by putting it out in the breeze and letting the pages flip to a certain place. Simply continue having your quiet time, reading and studying the Bible, and going to church, and let your heart go out to the Lord concerning your need. At some point in time—it may be a day or a week or a month or several months later—the Holy Spirit will impress you as you're moving through God's Word. And He'll say, "This is for you."

You've been presenting your needs to Him, and suddenly the Spirit of God witnesses to your heart and says, "Claim this promise in prayer." God has spoken to you.

Finally, remember that God makes and keeps promises for His glory—"that all the peoples of the earth may know that the Lord is God" (1 Kings 8:60).[1]

———◆———

ABOUT THE AUTHOR: Skip Gray has been a staff member of The Navigators for more than forty years, currently as part of the Business and Professional Ministry team. His primary focus is among physicians.

QUESTIONS FOR REFLECTION

1. Can we tend to "presume" upon God by loosely or inappropriately claiming His promises? Explain your thinking.

2. Concerning specific promises, which are the guidelines you're most prone to ignore? Which do you keep in mind?

▶ TIPS FOR DISCIPLING

Promises to Claim for a Disciple

by John D. Purvis

Here are some sample scriptural promises you can pray into the life of your disciple. The promises may apply to more than one category. It's very effective to compile your own list and to personalize your prayers considering your disciple's needs.

FOR HIS OR HER WALK WITH GOD

Matthew 11:28-30
"Come to me, all you who are weary and burdened, and I will give you rest. Take my yoke upon you and learn from me, for I am gentle and humble in heart, and you will find rest for your souls. For my yoke is easy and my burden is light."

John 15:5
"I am the vine; you are the branches. If a man remains in me and I in him, he will bear much fruit; apart from me you can do nothing."

FOR HIS OR HER CHARACTER

2 Peter 1:3-4
"His divine power has given us everything we need for life and godliness through our knowledge of him who called us by his own glory and goodness. Through these he has given us his very great and precious promises, so that through them you may participate in the divine nature and escape the corruption in the world caused by evil desires."

James 1:12
"Blessed is the man who perseveres under trial, because when he has stood the test, he will receive the crown of life that God has promised to those who love him."

FOR HIS OR HER RELATIONSHIPS

Philippians 4:6-7

"Do not be anxious about anything, but in everything, by prayer and petition, with thanksgiving, present your requests to God. And the peace of God, which transcends all understanding, will guard your hearts and your minds in Christ Jesus."

1 John 1:7

"But if we walk in the light, as he is in the light, we have fellowship with one another, and the blood of Jesus, his Son, purifies us from all sin."

FOR HIS OR HER WORK OR CAREER

Proverbs 3:5-6

"Trust in the LORD with all your heart and lean not on your own understanding; in all your ways acknowledge him, and he will make your paths straight."

Joshua 1:8

"Do not let this Book of the Law depart from your mouth; meditate on it day and night, so that you may be careful to do everything written in it. Then you will be prosperous and successful."

Proverbs 16:3

"Commit to the LORD whatever you do, and your plans will succeed."

FOR HIS OR HER MINISTRY

1 Corinthians 15:58

"Therefore, my dear brothers, stand firm. Let nothing move you. Always give yourselves fully to the work of the Lord, because you know that your labor in the Lord is not in vain."

John 12:24

"I tell you the truth, unless a kernel of wheat falls to the ground and dies, it remains only a single seed. But if it dies, it produces many seeds."

HABITS OF THE HEART

LESSON PLAN

- Share highlights from personal devotional lives.
- Review 1 Timothy 4:7-8.
- Discuss again "Rules for the Journey" on pages 20-21. Evaluate and make changes accordingly.
- Share ministry progress of potential disciples and issues you're facing.
- Discuss "Habits of the Heart" Bible study.
- Discuss articles on spiritual disciplines.
- Discuss Tips for Discipling: "Habits Make the Difference."

ASSIGNMENT FOR SESSION 9: THE PROCESS OF DISCIPLEMAKING

- Prepare the Bible study "The Process of Disciplemaking."
- Read the article "We're in This Together."
- Memorize Colossians 1:28-29.
- Continue personal devotional times.
- Meet with your growing disciples.
- Read Tips for Discipling: "Ways to Help an Apathetic Disciple."

GROUP PRAYER REQUESTS

► BIBLE STUDY

HABITS OF THE HEART

"Life without discipline is disaster." (Proverbs 25:28, paraphrase)

Gaining a correct perspective on spiritual disciplines isn't easy. Trying to walk the path of truth, we tend to err by going over the passivity cliff on one side or the legalism cliff on the other side. Richard Foster deals with this issue in his classic book on spiritual disciplines. Read the following paragraphs by Foster and highlight the ideas that stand out to you.

When we despair of gaining inner transformation through human powers of will and determination, we are open to a wonderful new realization: inner righteousness is a gift from God to be graciously received. The needed change within us is God's work, not ours. The demand is for an inside job, and only God can work from the inside. We cannot attain or earn this righteousness of the kingdom of God; it is a grace that is given.

In the book of Romans, the apostle Paul goes to great lengths to show that righteousness is a gift of God. He uses the term thirty-five times in this epistle and each time insists that righteousness is unattained and unattainable through human effort. One of the clearest statements is Romans 5:17, "Those who receive the abundance of grace and the free gift of righteousness [shall] reign in life through the one man Jesus Christ." This teaching, of course, is found not only in Romans but throughout Scripture and stands as one of the cornerstones of the Christian faith.

The moment we grasp this breathtaking insight we are in danger of an error in the opposite direction. We are tempted to believe there is nothing we can do. If all human strivings end in moral bankruptcy (and having tried it, we know it is so), and if righteousness is a gracious gift from God (as the Bible clearly states), then is it not logical to conclude that we must wait for God to come and transform us? Strangely enough, the answer is no. The analysis is correct—human striving is insufficient and righteousness is a gift from God but the conclusion is faulty. Happily, we can do something. We do not need to be hung on the horns of the dilemma of either human works or idleness. God has given us the Disciplines of the spiritual life as a means of receiving his grace. The Disciplines allow us to place ourselves before God so that he can transform us.

The apostle Paul says, "he who sows to his own flesh will from the flesh reap corruption; but he who sows to the Spirit will from the Spirit reap eternal life" (Galatians 6:8). Paul's analogy is instructive. A farmer is helpless to grow grain; all he can do is provide the right conditions for the growing of grain. He cultivates the ground, he plants the seed, he waters the plants, and then the natural forces of the earth take over and up comes the grain. This is the way it is with the Spiritual Disciplines; they are a way of sowing to the Spirit. The Disciplines are God's way of getting us into the ground; they put us where he can work within us and transform us. By themselves, the Spiritual Disciplines can do nothing; they can only get us to the place where something can be done. They are God's means of grace. The inner righteousness we seek is not something that is poured on our heads. God has ordained the Disciplines of the spiritual life as the means by which we place ourselves where he can bless us.[1]

Spiritual disciplines are what we do so God can do what we can't do.

DALLAS WILLARD

1. What does the concept "spiritual disciplines" mean to you?

R. Paul Stevens defines spiritual disciplines as the Christian practices that encourage spiritual growth and transformation.[2] Although Scripture doesn't give us a comprehensive list of spiritual disciplines, Foster categorizes some of the more classic spiritual disciplines in three areas:

The Inward Disciplines
   Meditation
   Prayer
   Fasting
   Study

The Outward Disciplines
   Simplicity
   Solitude
   Submission
   Service

The Corporate Disciplines
   Confession
   Worship
   Guidance
   Celebration

ATTITUDES AND THE CULTIVATION OF DISCIPLINES

Read Isaiah 58:1-14.

2a. What are the effects and results for those who have an improper attitude (verses 1-6)?

2b. What is the effect when people have a correct attitude (verses 7-14)?

   Discipline and *disciple* come from the same root word. *Exercise* comes from the Greek word *gumnasia* and is the source of our word *gymnasium;* it has to do with stripping down to practice. In biblical terminology, discipline means training or exercise.

2c. What do the following passages teach about spiritual training, practice, or exercise?
   Deuteronomy 6:5-8

   Luke 6:47-49

   1 Timothy 4:7-9

DISCIPLINE REQUIRES SELF-CONTROL AND DILIGENCE

   3. What do the following verses teach about the importance of training yourself in self-control?
   1 Corinthians 9:24-27

   1 Timothy 4:12-15

Hebrews 5:14–6:1

Hebrews 12:11

1 Peter 5:8-10

FREEDOM THROUGH DISCIPLINE

"Freedom is the final reward of discipline," said Elisabeth Elliot. She recognized that disciplines not only create the environment for God's Spirit to work but also lead us to greater freedom. Anyone who has persisted in discipline on the piano, for example, has greater freedom to play music than those who have never practiced.

One of the big reasons for developing habits or spiritual discipline is so we can respond to the immediate and unpredicted circumstances in our lives with the right actions. The "suddenlies" of life can make us or break us. How we act during an eventful two seconds could determine our whole destiny.

4a. In Daniel 6:3-10, how does Daniel illustrate the benefits of discipline?

4b. In Mark 14:37-38,69-72, how does Peter illustrate the need of discipline?

4c. What does Ephesians 6:13 teach about freedom and discipline?

4d. Summarize your thoughts on freedom and discipline.

Habits can turn harmful and become detrimental. Spiritually, this is referred to as "legalism."

5a. Read the following passages and finish this statement for each one: Habits or practices
   enslave us when . . .
   Isaiah 29:13

Matthew 7:1-5

Matthew 12:9-14

5b. How can we keep spiritual disciplines from evolving into enslaving customs?

BEING CAPTURED

What makes spiritual disciplines important is that they create an environment where God can capture and change our hearts.

> God does not take our spiritual temperature under the tongue by the words we say,
> nor in our ear by the impressive teachings we hear, nor under our arms by the service
> we perform. God takes our spiritual temperature straight from the heart.[3]
>
> BETH MOORE

6a. What do these passages teach us to avoid?
Matthew 15:1-9

Revelation 2:1-10

6b. How does the Holy Spirit help us?
John 14:26

1 Corinthians 2:9-12

Ephesians 1:17-19

DISTRACTIONS

One common difficulty is that we easily get distracted by various things: the tyranny of the urgent, busyness, the television or newspaper, the "do list." The list could go on and on. Spiritual disciplines can help bring focus into the complexities of our lives.

7a. What insight can you gain from the following definitions?

Distracted—having the attention diverted; rendered incapable of behaving, reacting, etc., in a normal manner, as by worry, remorse, or the like; irrational; disturbed; 1. not brought into focus; lacking proper focus; 2. lacking a clear purpose or direction
Synonyms: unfocused, preoccupied, side-tracked, diverted, troubled, unfocused

Preoccupied—1. completely engrossed in thought; absorbed; 2. previously occupied; taken; filled

Diverted—turned aside or from a path or course; deflected; drawn off to a different course, purpose, etc.; distracted from serious occupation; entertained or amused

7b. What do the following verses say about distractions?
Psalm 119:37

Proverbs 24:30-34

Luke 10:40-41

2 Corinthians 7:1

Hebrews 12:1-2

GRACE AND THE SPIRITUAL DISCIPLINES

8. What relationship do you see between effort and grace in the following passages?
1 Corinthians 15:10

2 Corinthians 12:9

Hebrews 12:15

2 Peter 3:18

Grace is not opposed to effort but to earning.

DALLAS WILLARD

SUMMARY

9. In what ways have you found discipline leading to freedom in your own life—either in the natural or in the spiritual environment?

10. What spiritual disciplines do you feel are foundational to becoming a mature disciple of Christ?

11. How are your spiritual disciplines currently? Which are strong? Weak?

12. What are some practical things you've learned to help you cultivate discipline or self-control?

A simple yet effective model for training others in the spiritual disciplines is:

- Tell them why.
- Show them how.
- Get them started.
- Keep them going.

The Spiritual Disciplines

by Donald Whitney

DISCIPLINE WITHOUT DIRECTION IS drudgery.

Imagine six-year-old Kevin, whose parents have enrolled him in music lessons. After school every afternoon, he sits in the living room and reluctantly strums "Home on the Range" while watching his buddies play baseball in the park across the street. That's discipline without direction. It's drudgery.

Now suppose Kevin is visited by an angel one afternoon during guitar practice. In a vision, he's taken to Carnegie Hall. He's shown a guitar virtuoso giving a concert. Usually bored by classical music, Kevin is astonished by what he sees and hears. The musician's fingers dance excitedly on the strings with fluidity and grace. Kevin thinks of how stupid and clunky his hands feel when they halt and stumble over the chords. The virtuoso blends clean, soaring notes into a musical aroma that wafts from his guitar. Kevin remembers the toneless, irritating discord that comes stumbling out of his.

But Kevin is enchanted. His head tilts slightly to one side as he listens. He drinks in everything. He never imagined that anyone could play the guitar like this.

"What do you think, Kevin?" asks the angel.

The answer is a soft, slow, six-year-old's "W-o-w!"

The vision vanishes, and the angel is again standing in front of Kevin in his living room. "Kevin," says the angel, "the wonderful musician you saw is you in a few years." Then pointing at the guitar, the angel declares, "But you must practice!"

Suddenly the angel disappears and Kevin finds himself alone with his guitar. Do you think his attitude toward practice will be different now? As long as he remembers what he's going to become, Kevin's discipline will have a direction, a goal that will pull him into the future. Yes, effort will be involved, but you could hardly call it drudgery.

When it comes to discipline in the Christian life, many believers feel as Kevin did toward guitar practice—it's discipline without direction. Prayer threatens to be drudgery. The practical value of meditation on Scripture seems uncertain. The real purpose of a Discipline like fasting is often unclear.

First, we must understand what we shall become. It is said of God's elect in Romans 8:29, "For those God foreknew he also predestined to be conformed to the image of his Son." God's eternal plan ensures that every Christian will ultimately conform to Christlikeness. We will be changed "when he appears" so that "we shall be like him" (1 John 3:2). This is no vision; this is you, Christian, in a few years.

So why all the talk about discipline? If God has predestined our conformity to Christlikeness, where does discipline fit in?

Although God will grant Christlikeness to us when Jesus returns, until then He intends for us to grow toward that Christlikeness. We aren't merely to wait for holiness; we're to pursue it. "Make every effort to live in peace with all men and to be holy," we're commanded in Hebrews 12:14, for "without holiness no one will see the Lord."

Which leads us to ask what every Christian should ask, "How then shall we pursue holiness? How can we be like Jesus Christ, the Son of God?"

We find a clear answer in 1 Timothy 4:7: "Discipline yourself for the purpose of godliness" (NASB).

THE MEANS TO GODLINESS

The Spiritual Disciplines are those personal and corporate disciplines that promote spiritual growth. They are the habits of devotion and experiential Christianity that have been practiced by the people of God since biblical times.

The Spiritual Disciplines are Bible intake, prayer, worship, evangelism, service, stewardship, fasting, silence and solitude, journaling, and learning. This is by no means an exhaustive list of the Disciplines of Christian living. A survey of other literature on this subject would reveal that confession, accountability, simplicity, submission, spiritual direction, celebration, affirmation, sacrifice, watching, and more also qualify as Spiritual Disciplines.

Whatever the Discipline, its most important feature is its purpose. Just as there is little value in practicing the scales on a guitar or piano apart from the purpose of playing music, there is little value in practicing Spiritual Disciplines apart from the single purpose that unites them (Colossians 2:20-23, 1 Timothy 4:8). That purpose is godliness. We are told in 1 Timothy 4:7 to discipline ourselves "for the purpose of godliness."

The Spiritual Disciplines are the God-given means we are to use in the Spirit-filled pursuit of godliness.

Godly people are disciplined people. It has always been so. Call to mind some heroes of church history—Augustine, Martin Luther, John Calvin, John Bunyan, Susanna Wesley, George Whitefield, Lady Huntingdon, Jonathan and Sarah Edwards, Charles Spurgeon, George Muller— they were all disciplined people. In my own pastoral and personal Christian experience, I can say that I've never known a man or woman who came to spiritual maturity except through discipline. Godliness comes through discipline.

Actually, God uses three primary catalysts for changing us and conforming us to Christlikeness, but only one is largely under our control. One catalyst the Lord uses to change us is people. "As iron sharpens iron, so one man sharpens another" (Proverbs 27:17). Sometimes God uses our friends to sharpen us into more Christlike living, and sometimes He uses our enemies to file away our rough, ungodly edges. Parents, children, spouses, coworkers, customers, teachers, neighbors, pastors—God changes us through these people.

Another change agent God uses in our lives is circumstances. The classic text for this is Romans 8:28: "We know that in all things God works for the good of those who love him, who have been called according to his purpose." Financial pressures, physical conditions, even the weather are used in the hands of Divine Providence to stimulate His elect toward holiness.

Then there is the catalyst of the Spiritual Disciplines. This catalyst differs from the first two in that when He uses the Disciplines, God works from the inside out. When He changes us through people and circumstances, the process works from the outside in. The Spiritual Disciplines also differ from the other two methods of change in that God grants us a measure of choice regarding involvement with them. We often have little choice regarding the people and circumstances God brings into our lives, but we can decide, for example, whether we will read the Bible or fast today.

So on the one hand, we recognize that even the most iron-willed self-discipline will not make us more holy, for growth in holiness is a gift from God (John 17:17, 1 Thessalonians 5:23, Hebrews 2:11). On the other hand, we can do something to further the process. God has given us the Spiritual Disciplines as a means of receiving His grace and growing in godliness. By them we place ourselves before God for Him to work in us.

The New Testament was first written in Greek. The word translated *discipline* in the New American Standard Bible is the Greek word *gumnasia* from which our English words *gymnasium* and *gymnastics* derive. This word means "to exercise or discipline," which is why the King James Version renders 1 Timothy 4:7, "Exercise thyself rather unto godliness."

Think of the Spiritual Disciplines as spiritual exercises. To go to your favorite spot for prayer or journaling, for example, is like going to a gym and using a weight machine. As physical disciplines like this promote strength, so the Spiritual Disciplines promote godliness.

There are two Bible stories that illustrate another way of thinking of the role of the Spiritual Disciplines. Luke 18:35-43 tells the story of a blind beggar named Bartimaeus and his encounter with Jesus. As Bartimaeus sat by a roadside near Jericho, a crowd of unusual numbers and excitement came near. When he asked what was happening, he was told that Jesus of Nazareth was passing by. Even a social outcast like Bartimaeus had heard the incredible stories about Jesus that had come from all over Israel during the past two or three years. Immediately, he began shouting, "Jesus, Son of David, have mercy on me!" Those who were leading the procession, perhaps some of the local dignitaries, were embarrassed by the beggar's disruptive behavior and sternly told him to keep quiet. But he only cried out all the more, "Jesus, Son of David, have mercy on me!" To everyone's amazement, Jesus stopped and called for the one who was calling for Him. In response to the poor man's faith, Jesus miraculously healed Bartimaeus of his blindness.

The second Bible story is in the very next paragraph of Scripture, Luke 19:1-10. It's the famous account of the conversion of the tax collector, Zacchaeus. Perhaps it happened only minutes after the healing of Bartimaeus. Because Zacchaeus was so short, he was unable to see Jesus in the crowd. So he ran ahead and climbed into a sycamore tree in order to see Jesus when He passed by it. When Jesus came to the place, He looked up, called Zacchaeus by name, and told him to come down. The two of them went to the tax collector's house, where he believed in Christ for salvation and resolved to give half his possessions to the poor and return with interest all tax money he had wrongfully taken.

Think of the Spiritual Disciplines as ways we can place ourselves in the path of God's grace and seek Him much as Bartimaeus and Zacchaeus placed themselves in Jesus' path and sought Him. As with these two seekers, we will find Him willing to have mercy on us and to have communion with us. And in the course of time we will be transformed by Him from one level of Christlikeness to another (2 Corinthians 3:18).

The Spiritual Disciplines then are also like channels of God's transforming grace. As we place ourselves in them to seek communion with Christ, His grace flows to us and we are changed. That's why the Disciplines must become priority for us if we will be godly.

The great British Baptist preacher of the nineteenth century, Charles Spurgeon, stressed the importance this way: "I must take care above all that I cultivate communion with Christ, for though that can never be the basis of my peace—mark that—yet it will be the channel of it." The channels of peace and all that Christ gives that lead us to holiness are the Spiritual Disciplines.

Tom Landry, coach of the Dallas Cowboys football team for most of three decades, said, "The job of a football coach is to make men do what they don't want to do in order to achieve what they've always wanted to be." In much the same way, Christians are called to make themselves do something they would not naturally do—pursue the Spiritual Disciplines—in order to become what they've always wanted to be, that is, like Jesus Christ. "Discipline yourself," says the Scriptures, "for the purpose of godliness."[4]

The Spiritual Disciplines

by Jerry Bridges

WHEN I WAS FIRST introduced to the idea of discipleship, I was given a list of seven spiritual disciplines I should practice every day—things such as a daily quiet time, Scripture memorization, Bible study, and prayer. As overwhelming as that list was, I did manage to survive and am extremely grateful for the spiritual disciplines I learned in the process. But I soon came to believe that my day-to-day relationship with God depended on how faithfully I performed those disciplines.

No one actually told me God's blessing on my life was based on my performance. Still, I had developed a vague but very real impression that God's smile or frown depended on what I did. The frequent challenge to "be faithful" in my quiet time, while intrinsically good, probably helped create this impression. Soon, I was passing on this legalistic attitude to those I was seeking to disciple.

In recent years I've noticed an even stronger emphasis on discipleship by legalism. Not only do some people convey that God's smile or frown is dependent on a person's performance, they communicate by attitude and action that their own approval is based on a person's faithful performance of certain disciplines or attendance at certain Christian activities. The message is: People who don't do these things faithfully are not as "spiritual" or "committed" as those who do.

However, it's not rules that effectively disciple a person, it's God's grace. As the Apostle Paul said, "For the grace of God that brings salvation has appeared to all men. It teaches us to say 'No' to ungodliness and worldly passions, and to live self-controlled, upright and godly lives in this present age" (Titus 2:11-12).

Note that Paul says it is the grace of God—not a regimen of rules and activities—that teaches or disciples us. If we want to disciple others in a biblical manner, we must disciple by the grace of God, not by legalism. But this poses a problem.

PROCLAIM THE GOOD NEWS

Too many people set grace and discipline (or discipleship) in opposition to one other. Just as there is a strong element of legalistic discipleship within evangelicalism, there is an equally strong element of teaching that any emphasis on spiritual disciplines is a negation of God's grace.

How then can we apply Titus 2:11-12 in our discipling ministries? How can we disciple by grace? First, we must continue to teach the Gospel to the people we are discipling. Our tendency is to proclaim this "Good News" to people until they trust Christ; then we begin to teach them the demands of discipleship. But the Gospel is the Good News that God sent His Son into the world to die for all our sins—not just the sins we committed before we trusted Christ, but all our sins past, present, and future.

What do I mean when I say we must continue to preach the Gospel to Christians? A believer recently said to a friend of mine, "I'm a failure." In an effort to encourage, my friend told this person, "No, you're not a failure." While I appreciate my friend's compassion, I would suggest a different response to such a statement and the attitude of despair lying behind it. I would suggest that we say something like this: "That's right. You are a failure, and so am I. But that's why Jesus came. He came to die for people who are failures." You see, this dear person needed to hear the Gospel just as much that day as she did the day she trusted Christ as her Savior.

Jesus came for spiritual failures, not for the spiritually successful. He said, "It is not the healthy who need a doctor, but the sick. I have not come to call the righteous [the spiritually successful], but sinners [the spiritual failures] to repentance'" (Luke 5:31-32). We don't like to admit we're failures, but we really are! Jesus said we are to love the Lord our God with all our heart, soul, and mind, and to love our neighbor as ourselves (Matthew 22:37-38). By that standard, all of us are failures. None of us has even come close to loving God with all our hearts and our neighbors as ourselves.

MERIT IS SPELLED G-R-A-C-E

I believe the two greatest hindrances to discipleship are self-righteousness and guilt. Some people aren't interested in pursuing true biblical discipleship because they're satisfied with their own performance. They've reduced the Christian life to measurable activities. Supposedly, they are the spiritually healthy Jesus spoke of who don't need the doctor (Luke 5:31-32).

Other believers are weighed down with guilt—often about the wrong things. They worry that they haven't succeeded in the spiritual disciplines as others seem to have done, or they've truly failed in a significant area of their lives and feel guilty about it. They haven't yet learned that Jesus died for those who have failed.

The Gospel strips us of self-righteousness and frees us from guilt. The Gospel, reiterated every day, reminds the seemingly "successful" disciple that he really is a sinner because "no sinner, no Savior." It reminds the seemingly "unsuccessful" disciple that Jesus died for all his failures to practice the disciplines of discipleship.

Once a person is able to put his failures into perspective, what next? We must help those we disciple realize that even their most diligent pursuit of spiritual disciplines never earns them one iota of favor from God. God's blessings come to us by His grace—through the merit of Jesus Christ. God's grace has been defined through the acrostic G-R-A-C-E, "God's Riches At Christ's Expense." This means that Jesus Christ has already merited for us every blessing and every answer to prayer we will ever receive. The practical outworking of this truth means that when I am "faithful" in my quiet time, I do not earn God's blessing. Conversely, when I haven't been faithful I haven't forfeited God's blessing.

This truth needs to be emphasized over and over, because we're all legalistic by nature. We don't have to be taught to relate to God on a performance basis; we do that naturally. Rather, we have to be taught over and over again that the only way we can truly relate to God is by His grace, through the merit of Jesus Christ. Why, then, should we be concerned with the practice of spiritual disciplines?

THE WAY TO SPIRITUAL HEALTH

Although the spiritual disciplines don't earn God's favor, they're absolutely necessary for spiritual growth.

An analogy I sometimes use is that of a child eating the nutritious food his mother has prepared. Eating the food doesn't earn his mother's approval (though she is undoubtedly pleased that he's eating it), but it is vitally necessary for his physical growth and health. In the same way, practicing spiritual disciplines doesn't earn God's approval (though He is pleased), but it is vitally necessary for our spiritual growth.

Exposure to the truths of God's Word through the teaching of others and our own personal study, consistent prayer, and the fellowship of other believers are some of the basic disciplines God has given us for our spiritual growth. We simply won't grow without consistency in these disciplines any more than a child will grow healthily apart from nutritious food. It's not an issue of God's approval or disapproval (and should not be a matter of our approval or disapproval). It's simply an issue of growth.

GRACE DOES NOT EQUAL INDULGENCE

But suppose people don't want to grow or, perhaps more accurately, don't want to pay the price of the spiritual disciplines necessary to grow. What do we do then? We do what Paul did. We admonish and teach (Colossians 1:28). We warn them of the dangers of spiritual slothfulness. We teach them the true meaning and intent of the grace of God as portrayed, for example, in Titus 2:11-12. We point out that Jesus died, not just to rescue us from eternal damnation but "to redeem us from all wickedness and to purify for Himself a people that are His very own, eager to do what is good" (Titus 2:14).

All the while we are admonishing and teaching, we should do so with an attitude of total acceptance. We should never imply to those we're discipling that God's favor is dependent on their faithfulness; rather, it's based on the merit of Jesus Christ on their behalf. And we should certainly never indicate by our attitude or actions that our acceptance of them is based on their performance.

But doesn't this teaching of God's unconditional love to us in Christ lead to a careless attitude on the part of some? Yes it does—sometimes even to the point of willful and flagrant disobedience. To these people we must emphasize that God's grace doesn't negate the scriptural principles that "a man reaps what he sows" (Galatians 6:7), and "The Lord disciplines those He loves" (Hebrews 12:6). God's unconditional love should never be equated with permissiveness and indulgence.

Likewise, our love should be unconditional yet not permissive. It should be like Paul's love as expressed to the Corinthians, "For I wrote you out of great distress and anguish of heart and with many tears, not to grieve you but to let you know the depth of my love for you" (2 Corinthians 2:4).

In all of our discipling relationships, we must remember that we are only ministers of God. If God accepts a person by His grace, we must accept a person on the same basis, loving him unconditionally but not permissively. The foundation of our discipling should be the Gospel, not the spiritual disciplines. Only a person who is firmly established in the Gospel can handle the important disciplines of the Christian life without falling into legalism.[5]

Spiritual Disciplines

by Alan Andrews

THIS WEEK I WAS reflecting on the idea of spiritual disciplines. After all, words like *discipline* go against the grain of postmodernism and our convenience-oriented culture. Since Navigators have long been known for their practice of spiritual disciplines (the basics), they're something that we all think about and spend a lot of time practicing.

Last year, I read Dallas Willard's *Divine Conspiracy* again. In this book, Willard talks a good deal about how the world that we experience with our senses isn't the real world. The real world is the Kingdom of God. One of the difficulties that we and those we minister to face is that the world perceived by our senses is in conflict with the real world that God inaugurated with the Lord Jesus. Keeping our minds, thoughts, and actions centered on the real world requires a lot of work.

That's where the spiritual disciplines can really serve us. Willard sees the disciplines as tools or means of allowing the grace of God to flow in our lives. The disciplines don't allow us to earn favor with God, but rather increasingly help tame our minds and our bodies (hand-in-hand with the Spirit) so that we can grow in "offering our bodies as living sacrifices" (Romans 12:1). But the value of the disciplines will only be felt when they're entered into with the right mindset: "They are self-confirming when entered into in faith and humility," Willard says. "And you don't really need much faith and humility if you will just stay with them. They will do the rest because they open us to the kingdom."

So where should we start? I appreciate how Willard breaks the disciplines into two main categories: abstinence and action. Some of the examples of abstinence are solitude (it is essential to be outside of human contact for long periods of time in order to give our flesh time to stop responding at the "epidermal" level), silence (quietness, even from our own voice), and others I would add include fasting (learning that it is not food that satisfies and fills us) and rest (stopping activity and being still to hear the Lord Jesus). We need to practice disciplines of abstinence in order to free ourselves from the constant input of the false reality the world conveys to us.

We tend to be more familiar with the action disciplines. Study, Scripture memory, and meditation are essential not simply to increase our knowledge or to feel closer to God, but also so we can internalize the order and nature of the Kingdom into our thoughts, feelings, and ultimately our actions. If the abstaining disciplines purify our minds and hearts of the world's reality, then study (and the other action disciplines like worship and prayer) fills us with the true reality of God's presence in our lives.

Our world is moving farther and farther from the reality of the reign and rule of God. In this postmodern and post-Christian time we live in, the disciplines (the basics) are probably more valuable and necessary now than ever before.[6]

QUESTIONS FOR REFLECTION

1. How do you explain the relationship between grace and discipline?
2. How would you explain the importance of spiritual disciplines to a growing disciple?

▶ TIPS FOR DISCIPLING

Habits Make the Difference

by Randy D. Raysbrook

Don't get frustrated the next time your disciple fails to be as disciplined as you would like him or her to be. Instead, use these suggestions to develop godly habits in both yourself and others.

What separates great men and women of God from believers who fade into history, leaving scarcely a mark on anyone's life? At least part of the difference is in their habits. People who influence others have become proficient in the "basics." They determine what patterns are necessary to maintain intimacy with Christ and they make those a priority in their lives. God designed us so that, when we're not up to full strength, the habit patterns we build into our lives can begin to take over. "Since habits become power," wrote E. Stanley Jones, "make them work with you, not against you."

Habits in the basics are important because:

- They serve God. God is worthy of our continual attention. Habits keep us focused on Him.
- They help us. Only through regular time with the Lord, with His Word, and with His people can we experience the fullness of life Jesus promises in John 10:10.
- They help others. We can't help meet others' needs unless we're growing in our intimacy with the Lord. Through intimacy with God we find the grace, strength, and insights necessary to love others. Our love for others demands that we discipline ourselves.

Here are ten ways to help you develop habits in the basics. Model and explain them to the disciples you're training.

1. MAKE A DECISION

Our Christian life is a tapestry woven with the threads of daily decisions. J. Oswald Sanders reminded us that we self-classify in the Christian life: The choice is ours. We are what we choose. So the starting place for a life of godly consistency is always the decisions we make. For example, a morning quiet time is a choice: mind over mattress. Our feelings aren't the issue. A person driving to San Francisco fills his car with gasoline when it needs it, not when he feels like doing it. Likewise, we regularly need to meet certain needs in our spiritual lives whether or not we feel like meeting them. Emotions are servants of the mind, and the mind is the servant of the will. We must often choose against self in order to choose God.

2. BE ACCOUNTABLE TO OTHERS

Being accountable to others protects us from our natural weaknesses and allows us to minister to others as they become a part of our growth. Accountability means inviting another to ask you questions about your walk with God and your life. Your life becomes an open book for joint discussion. Discipleship is about pilgrims on the same journey encouraging, strengthening, and loving one another. This needs to be done creatively, however. You need to customize the exact method of accountability you use to the personality and needs of the individuals. Everyone is different—one size does not fit all.

3. START WITH A SYSTEM

Whatever spiritual discipline you're working on, try to find a regular system that others have used successfully. In Scripture memory, for example, The Navigators' Topical Memory System promotes consistent progress in Scripture memorization and review. There are also a number of excellent discipleship Bible study tools and materials available. Starting a new disciple with a system gives that person predictability and structure and these help develop lifetime habits. Eventually you may choose to create your own systems. If so, keep them simple and evaluate them regularly to make sure they build your consistency and move you toward the goal of Christlikeness.

4. REMEMBER GRANDMA'S LAW

Do you remember when you were younger and your grandmother promised you some apple pie if you ate all your spinach? That's Grandma's Law. We can use the same principle to motivate ourselves and others. Many have adopted the motto, "No Bible, no breakfast." A friend of mine allowed himself to watch television for only as much time as he had spent reading and studying the Bible.

5. IMPROVISE

If you missed your scheduled prayer time this morning, don't think you've blown the day and can't recover. Improvise and break your prayer time into several short segments that you can include throughout the day's schedule. You can always find creative ways to discipline yourself for purposes of godliness (1 Timothy 4:7).

6. USE ASSOCIATION

I have a friend who committed himself to pray for me daily. He does so as he takes his daily thyroid pill. By linking his prayer with his pill he'll always remember to pray for me. I know of students who pray on campus each time they hear the class buzzers ring. You can also use landmarks that you pass on your way to work each day as a cue for praying or for reviewing memorized verses.

7. START SMALL AND BUILD

Your goal is consistency, not quantity. Start with a small, manageable goal, and build up from there. A goal too low is better than one too high. You can always increase your goal later, but if you set it too high and fail, your discouragement may hinder further growth. "Hope deferred makes the heart sick" (Proverbs 13:12).

8. IF YOU FAIL, PRESS ON

When we fail, Satan will draw our attention to our inadequacy, but Christ always draws our attention to His adequacy. If you become undisciplined, acknowledge it in prayer, ask in faith for the Lord's help to change, and press on. Proverbs 24:16 says, "For though a righteous man falls seven times, he rises again."

9. START WITH ONE AREA AT A TIME

I suggest that the first spiritual discipline you tackle should be a regular quiet time or a Scripture memory program. As you develop consistency in this area and begin to experience greater intimacy with the Lord, expand into other areas. Don't try to work on everything at once. God can guide you through prayer and His Word as you grow in other spiritual disciplines.

10. BE WILLING TO PAY THE PRICE

No pain, no gain. Godliness will cost us, but if it didn't cost anything it wouldn't be worth anything. "One of the mysteries of living," said Ted Engstrom, "is that that which is easily achieved brings little inner satisfaction."

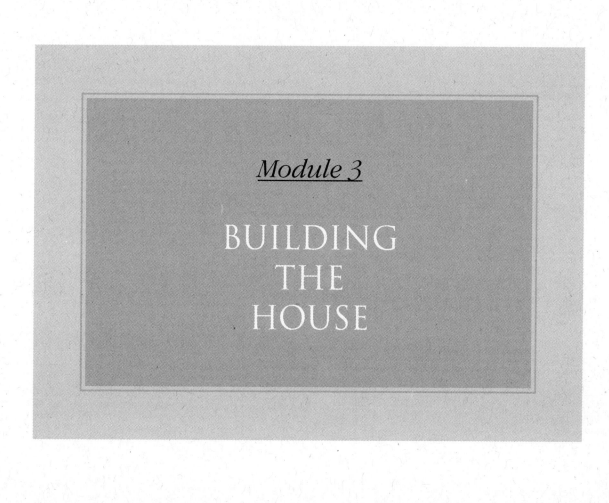

Module 3

BUILDING
THE
HOUSE

THE PROCESS OF DISCIPLEMAKING

LESSON PLAN

- Review Colossians 1:28-29.
- Share highlights from personal devotional times.
- Discuss the "The Process of Disciplemaking" Bible study.
- Share key ministry joys and concerns. Share how the growing disciples are demonstrating a heart for the Word.
- Pray as a group for each person you are discipling.
- Discuss the article "We're in This Together."
- Discuss Tips for Discipling: "Ways to Help an Apathetic Disciple."

ASSIGNMENT FOR SESSION 10: THE IMPORTANCE OF THE WORD

- Prepare the Bible study "The Importance of the Word."
- Read the article "Speaking God's Language."
- Memorize 2 Timothy 3:16-17.
- Review past Scripture memory verses.
- Continue personal devotional times.
- Read Tips for Discipling: "How to Pray for Your Disciple Using the Scriptures."
- Continue meeting with your growing disciples.

GROUP PRAYER REQUESTS

► BIBLE STUDY

THE PROCESS OF DISCIPLEMAKING

KEY ISSUES
- What are some interrelationships between discipleship and transformation?
- What are the key ingredients critical to the discipleship process?

The discipleship process isn't a series of events, but it *is* a journey. It includes a systematic series of actions directed toward walking with Christ in a deepening intimacy that results in becoming like Him. Similar to the growth of a child, it does involve stages.

Finish the following statement: "If disciples are made not born, then . . . "

TRANSFORMATION

Too often the Christian life is viewed as a ticket to heaven rather than a journey of transformation. "Change" is the fine print in the contract that we forgot to read. Being adopted into God's family, having our sins forgiven, and receiving a new status as joint heirs with Christ is certainly part of the gift. But following Christ demands change—change that comes from the inside out. Change involves more than acquiring a new worldview or theology. It involves our mind, emotions, and will. It affects our behavior, values, and core beliefs. Conformity to the image of Christ is the journey of discipleship.

The word *transform* comes from the Greek *metamorphoo* where we get our word *morph*. The picture in nature is of a caterpillar changing (morphing) into a butterfly.

1a. The following verses use the word *transform*. What observations can you make from these verses regarding the change process?
   Romans 12:1-3

   2 Corinthians 3:18

Philippians 3:21

1b. Read 1 Thessalonians 1. Note the correlation between life change and its impact.

1c. How have you experienced the transformation process during your spiritual journey?

1d. Which areas change more slowly than you would like?

1e. Who or what in the following verses is the change agent? What's our part? What are the results?
Ezekiel 18:31

Ezekiel 36:26

Romans 13:14

1 Corinthians 15:51-54

2 Corinthians 4:16

Ephesians 4:22-24

Colossians 3:9-10

1 Thessalonians 4:3

Titus 3:5

1 Peter 1:14-16

1f. Summarize into one statement the main ideas regarding transformation.

MODELS DESCRIBING THE DISCIPLESHIP PROCESS

PHYSICAL MODEL

I am writing to you, *little children*, because your sins are forgiven you for His name's sake. I am writing to you, *fathers,* because you know Him who has been from the beginning. I am writing to you, *young men,* because you have overcome the evil one. I have written to you, *children,* because you know the Father. I have written to you, *fathers,* because you know Him who has been from the beginning. I have written to you, *young men,* because you are strong, and the word of God abides in you, and you have overcome the evil one. (1 John 2:12-14, NASB, emphasis added)

Maturing through the physical stages of growth involves change. It's not easy to draw a conclusive line as to when one passes from one stage to the other but there are some indicators.

2a. From the previous passage, what are the maturity indicators for each stage of maturity? Add others you think are important.
Spiritual child/children

Spiritual young men/adult

Spiritual father/parent

GOSPEL MODEL

In his book *Jesus Christ Disciple Maker,* Bill Hull observes that in the training of the Twelve there were four phases of the process.

Phase 1: Come and See (John 1:35-39)
Phase 2: Follow Me (Matthew 4:19)
Phase 3: Be with Me (Mark 3:14)
Phase 4: Remain in Me (John 15:7-8)[1]

2b. How did Christ's training of the Twelve change over time?

2c. What changes do you observe in the apostles over time?

DIAMOND MODEL

A diamond can serve as a graphic to illustrate the process of maturity. With this model, the process is illustrated in four phases with corresponding results:

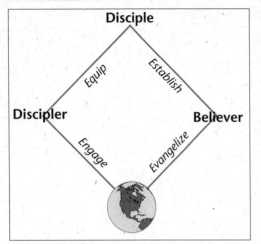

1. Evangelize to develop a believer.
2. Establish to develop a disciple.
3. Equip to develop a discipler.
4. Engage to develop an ambassador.

Notice that the process starts in the world and returns to the world. Discipling others should result in reaching others for Christ.

Each phase builds on the foundation of the previous one. The phases aren't sequential but cumulative. Just like becoming a parent adds to the maturity stage of an adult, so becoming a discipler adds to the maturity stage of a disciple. We don't leave one phase as we mature to another. We're always children of God even when we become spiritual parents.

RACE METAPHOR

There is also an athletic metaphor for the maturing process.

2d. What observations do you make from these verses regarding the essentials for a successful spiritual race or process?
Hebrews 12:1-3

1 Corinthians 9:24-27

2e. Summarize key ideas from these models.

INGREDIENTS FOR THE GROWTH PROCESS

What does it take to develop maturity? Although a precise formula for growth is difficult to form, we can identify key ingredients.

3a. What are some of the more obvious ingredients from the following verses?

Proverbs 27:17

John 14:21

John 17:17

Romans 8:28

2 Corinthians 12:9-10

Galatians 3:3

Ephesians 3:14-16

1 Thessalonians 5:23

Hebrews 5:12

Hebrews 12:11

3b. What would you say has been a key ingredient during your greatest periods of spiritual growth?

3c. What ingredients do you think are currently important for those you're discipling?

SUMMARY

4. What do these verses say is God's part and your part in the spiritual transformation process?
Luke 24:25-26,31-32,45

Ephesians 1:18-19

Philippians 2:12-13

Hebrews 3:8,12

5. How will your study of the discipling process affect how you disciple others?

Our risen Christ left this legacy—the Magna Charta of the church—"make disciples."
He provided both the model and the method. His life—and death—recast the lives of
men. He demonstrated that you have not done anything until you have changed the
lives of men.

HOWARD HENDRICKS

We're in This Together

by Robert N. Nielsen

*Discipleship isn't something we do to people as much
as it's something we are with them.*

THE RACE WAS ON. My two brothers, Tom and Mike, plummeted down the river ahead of me,
splashing and yelling their way to the best fishing spot. I was last out of the car. By the time I got
to the river, after tripping over my sneakers several times, they were long gone.

After several vain attempts to bushwhack some unsuspecting brook trout, I threw down my fishing rod on the bank and stormed off. As I stumbled through the brush back to where Dad was, I was sure there wasn't one friendly trout in that whole stream.

Pop had moved about a hundred feet from the point where he'd entered the river. He was peacefully standing shin-deep in the stream with a half-lit cigarette smoking out the side of his mouth, his rod and line working the swirling fishing pools in a lazy, unhurried manner. I wandered up behind him, complaining under my breath.

"There's no fish in there," I muttered, looking down.

"Oh, really?" He smiled as he lifted the top of his fishing creel. One look in the basket brought a squeal out of me. It was almost full of brookies.

"Where did you get those?" I asked with wide eyes.

"Shhhh!" he said. "Look down at your feet. Now tell me, where would you live if you were a hungry fish?"

"Where the food is, of course."

"Look at that rock right there. See the way the water curls around it? If I were a fish, I would wait just on the other side of that rock for a fat worm to float by. Why don't you try it?"

"Okay, but I already tried there, and there's no fish!"

You know the end of the story. The worm didn't have a chance. The hungry trout gulped him down and I pulled in my first fish of the trip, along with a lesson I'll never forget.

This was also my first lesson in discipling, angler style. Times like this fishing trip taught me that discipleship means relationship. There's no better way to learn to catch crafty brookies than by standing next to someone who has already outsmarted them. Of course, discipling isn't a process of outsmarting and catching people. But it's the process of getting close enough to people to share your life by example. Sharing by example became part of me early in life, and this life-to-life discipling process carried into my days as a student-discipler at college.

LIFE-TO-LIFE DISCIPLING

What started out in November 1980 as a dinner conversation about the dangers of hell, slowly and sometimes painfully matured into a committed lifetime friendship between Don and me—with Jesus in the middle.

We began to meet formally as well as informally. We spent a great deal of time together, winning a dorm basketball championship, talking late at night, complaining about the cafeteria food, and just clowning around. We tried to lead people to Jesus, we talked about our mutual struggles with sexual purity, and we often expressed our brotherly affection for one another. We eventually moved to another city together to start a new ministry. I have few friends who know me the way Don does.

Since those school days, Don moved to another city, met and married Abigail, and pursued a career in teaching. I don't see them as often as I'd like, but our lives are inextricably woven together with transparency, commitment, and honesty.

Over the last fifteen years of discipling others, certain things have become very apparent to me: People change because they want to change; they don't usually need more knowledge; and the barrier to someone becoming more like Christ is much more emotional and spiritual than it is intellectual. Therefore, discipleship is a process that needs to be deeply contextualized by relationship rather than by the passing on of facts. Discipleship isn't something we can do to someone as much as it is something we can be with that person. This distinction affects how I view my role as a discipler.

The old cliché that something is "caught rather than taught" is still true. We encourage people to grow by both the context of what we say as well as the content of what we teach. It's hard to find the balance, but it's wonderfully illustrated by the Apostle Paul's life.

PAUL, THE MISSIONARY MENTOR

Paul's balanced approach to discipling is clearly illustrated in 1 Thessalonians 2. Paul showed his love for the Thessalonians not only by the truth he taught them, but by the depth and purity of his friendship.

In 1 Thessalonians 2:3-5, Paul affirms his motives for befriending the Thessalonians. He wanted to please God, not people. He was being who God wanted him to be, and doing what God wanted him to do.

Within that context, Paul could give not only the truth of the Gospel but his whole life because of his love for them (1 Thessalonians 2:7-8). He fathered and mothered them—caring, exhorting, encouraging, and imploring each one. From a biblical perspective, truth delivered within a loving relationship is always the best balance.

A MATTER OF TRUST

Why is it so important for discipleship to be more than imparting knowledge or defining principles? Here are two answers I've discovered as I've worked with people.

PEOPLE NEED CONGRUENCE

In Nonverbal Communication 101, I learned that when a person gives two messages, a verbal and a nonverbal, the nonverbal is usually the true one. For instance, if I grimace when I say, "I love you," you'd probably question the sincerity of my words. When this double message happens in the discipling process, the disciple doesn't trust the process or the discipler.

This doesn't mean that the discipler has to be perfect or hide any struggles he or she may be going through. In fact, the more we reveal of ourselves, the more we demonstrate integrity and have a greater impact in the lives of others.

That's why it's essential that people see our failures. If they don't, they'll suspect something is wrong, either with us or with them. They know how full of failure their own lives are, so if they don't see all sides of us, they either believe we have a magic formula that they need to find, or they intuitively know we aren't as perfect as we appear.

When people see us fail and still grow, it frees them to do the same. It unlocks their emotional chains of fear and pride and propels them forward to new arenas of life.

When I met Paul Drake, he was a hard-driving ex-Marine. He seemed to communicate by his words and life that success as a Christian meant being just as disciplined and hard hitting as the Marines. This was an unrestrained type of faith without a lot of compassion. Frankly, it wasn't very appealing to me, but God was about to intervene.

During the next year, God used some wrenching medical problems in his dear wife, Georgia, to soften Paul's tempered-steel heart. Georgia's pain was the hammer God used in Paul's life. Today, he's one of the most compassionate, godly men I know. By watching this process of failure and change in his life, I was convinced that I could change, too.

As disciplers, we need to consciously give those we disciple an inside look, at both our successes and our failures. This integrity and congruence provide a tremendous platform for change in their lives.

GIVING AND RECEIVING

Another aspect of discipling that goes hand in hand with an inside look is allowing the disciple to give. This means that the discipler is willing to be taught by the disciple.

As "receptive disciplers," we're called to be vulnerable and needy, while remaining, in some ways, authority figures. Unlike the traditional instructor, who tends to be aloof and uninvolved, we let the disciples know we're "in process" just like them. We must swallow a "humility pill" when we admit we don't know it all and can learn great spiritual and practical lessons from our students. However, both student and teacher grow when we allow the student to give.

Helping Brian in his spiritual life encouraged me just because of who he was. Nevertheless, the day I decided to let him teach me about his passion—falconry—was a turning point in our relationship. Brian is a master falconer, and the process of becoming a falconer myself gave us a lot of time together. We spent hours out in the fields working with birds and learning the nuances of leather harnesses. This was time that Brian gave to me, and it allowed him to feel greater freedom and depth to share other areas of his life as well as offer input in the weak areas of my life.

CREATING A CONTEXT FOR CHANGE

In addition to transparency and teachability, a discipler has to create a context in which people want to change. This context is love. Sometimes people simply need help in figuring things out. Or they need encouragement to take risks.

When I first met Greg, he was a tall, rather clumsy new believer I'd begun to encourage in his faith. He was also vulnerable to being embarrassed. One day, the inevitable happened during a soccer game with some other Christians. Greg was humiliated and hurt because of his clumsiness in the midst of some robust action.

As Greg and I peeled rubber away from the soccer field in his red Camaro, Greg cursing like the proverbial sailor, all the Christian soccer players stared after us in disbelief. I wasn't sure if I really wanted to be sitting in this car either. Thankfully, we came to a dusty stop at an A&W root beer stand. We started yelling at each other, and eventually we cried. I had no idea how to help this guy, but I knew that I loved him. Therefore, that's what I told him.

This was a turning point in our relationship. By knowing he was loved when he felt least lovable, Greg was freed to be more honest with me and to make additional changes in his life.

THE COST OF DISCIPLING

Life-to-life discipling is expensive. It means that the discipler has to be more committed to the painful process of change in his or her own life than to seeing change take place in others. It won't work to say "do as I say, not as I do." It means that we're involved with other people not to avoid our own need for change or to gain self-esteem, but because we love God.

It also means investing time and adjusting our lifestyles. That includes making time when they're available, especially if they have a demanding job. Three days a week, I meet with businessmen as early as 6 A.M. The people at the Coco's restaurant down the street reserve a particular booth every Thursday morning. It's not my favorite time of the day to challenge traffic (California is notorious for its 6:30 A.M. urban rush), but it's the time when busy people are free. So that's the time we meet.

Discipling life-to-life also brings with it the possibility of disappointment.

My college roommate, whom I'd led to the Lord, moved out of our room six weeks into the semester. He was fed up with the pressure of living with a "Jesus freak" like me. His quick exit made it hard for me to live with myself for quite a while. There were nights of self-doubt and guilt, wondering if I'd damaged him and contributed to his hard heart. His new friends openly disliked me and drew pagan symbols on the door of my dorm room.

My ex-roommate's rebellion eventually led him to return to drugs and leave school. Late one night, however, I was awakened by garbled yelling and pounding on my door, and we rushed him, in his drugged stupor, to an emergency room to get his stomach pumped.

It was encouraging to know that he trusted me enough to come for help. But I often grieved that he never followed the Lord after that.

Getting involved in people's lives rather than simply imparting information opens us up to real pain. When we love much and we grow with the people we're helping, it's even more painful if they choose to stop growing and changing.

Life-to-life discipling has given me great rewards over the years, and I wouldn't trade my experiences for anything. It does involve a sacrifice of everything we are. Like the Apostle Paul, we need to be willing to give "not only the gospel of God but also our own lives."

We can give our lives to others only in the context of being in relationship with them. That's what I caught, along with brook trout, on my fishing trips with Pop—a concept of delivering truth in the context of relationships. If you can do that while getting some good fishing time on a cold stream, more power to you![2]

---◆---

ABOUT THE AUTHOR: Robert N. Nielson is a carpenter and freelance writer living in Campbell, California. He attends an Evangelical Free church in San Jose, where he's involved in the music ministry and in an outreach called Marketplace Ministry. He says that his best friends are creative, genuine, and tell him the truth. Someday he'd like to sail around the world in a three-masted schooner.

QUESTIONS FOR REFLECTION

1. Can you recall an instance when you learned an important lesson by example—"something caught rather than taught"?
2. Why do you think we tend to hide our shortcomings and failures?
3. Discipling means adjusting our lifestyles even when that's painful. What's one painful adjustment you've made since beginning to disciple others?

▶ TIPS FOR DISCIPLING

Ways to Help an Apathetic Disciple

by Rebecca Livermore

In spite of our best efforts, we'll all have times when apathy attacks the people we disciple. Their consistent quiet times may falter. They may fail to complete their Bible studies, make excuses for not attending, or show up but refuse to participate. Their zeal for witnessing may fade. After a time, they may even avoid you—refusing to return your phone calls and expressing irritation when you reach out to them.

Hebrews 10:24-25 exhorts us to consider how to spur one another on toward love and good deeds. Prayer is one of the best ways to spur on an apathetic disciple. Pray, as Paul did in Ephesians 1:17-19, that "the eyes of [their] heart may be enlightened in order that [they] may know the hope to which he has called [them], the riches of his glorious inheritance in the saints, and his incomparably great power for us who believe." Colossians 1:9-12 is another good passage of Scripture to pray.

SOMETIMES APATHY IS THE RESULT OF FATIGUE

If you think this might be the case, say, like Jesus said to His disciples in Mark 6:31, "Come with me by yourselves to a quiet place and get some rest." Take a weekend retreat together. Drop the agenda, the Scripture memory cards, and the Bible study. Walk and talk. Read. Pray—together or apart. Sit in silence. Listen to relaxing music. If all your companion wants to do is sleep, let him or her sleep. Your objective is rest, whatever form that takes.

SOMETIMES APATHY ARISES FROM LACK OF FOCUS

Hebrews 12:3 gives us a secret to perseverance: "Consider him who endured such opposition from sinful men, so that you will not grow weary and lose heart." Sometimes when we're discipling people, we try to feed them so much so fast that they can't absorb it all. Simplify your focus and theirs by setting aside all other objectives in order to concentrate on Jesus. Together, study His life. Talk about how His example inspires you to press on.

When apathy strikes, lower your expectations, offer the gift of rest, lean on God through prayer, and focus on the source of the life within you.[3]

THE IMPORTANCE OF THE WORD

LESSON PLAN

- Review 2 Timothy 3:16-17 and other Scripture memory verses.
- Share highlights from personal devotional times.
- Discuss the Bible study "The Importance of the Word."
- Share what marks of a disciple those you're discipling are demonstrating.
- Pray as a group for each person you are discipling.
- Discuss the article "Speaking God's Language."
- Discuss Tips for Discipling: "How to Pray for Your Disciple Using the Scriptures."

ASSIGNMENT FOR SESSION 11: THE VALUE OF EACH INDIVIDUAL

- Prepare the Bible study "The Value of Each Individual."
- Read the article "The Importance of Every Individual."
- Memorize Isaiah 60:22.
- Review past Scripture memory verses.
- Continue personal devotional times.
- Read Tips for Discipling: "Don't Give Up Yet."
- Continue to meet with your growing disciple(s).

GROUP PRAYER REQUESTS

▶ BIBLE STUDY

THE IMPORTANCE OF THE WORD

KEY ISSUES

- Are the Scriptures the only sure foundation for life and ministry?
- What does the Bible say about its authority and sufficiency?
- How can you plant God's Word deeply within the heart of a new disciple?

INTRODUCTION

When helping establish new believers, nothing's more critical in their relationships to Christ than grounding them in the Word. Peter implies that an appetite for the Word of God is an indicator of new birth: "Like newborn babies, crave pure spiritual milk, so that by it you may grow up in your salvation" (1 Peter 2:2).

A hunger for the Word is essential for healthy growth and life. Many substitutes exist, but nothing brings nourishment to life like God's Word. To many, the Scriptures are a nice option, a historic book, or a religious construct. We can't assume that new believers hold to a view of the authority and sufficiency of Scripture. They often begin their spiritual journey biblically illiterate or with misconceptions of what truths the Bible contains.

They may be coming from a view of life that says all truth is relative—that there are no absolutes. For them, the Bible is one of many sources, but not the authority for their life and practice. As you disciple others, you need to make two things evident:

1. Scripture is your authority in life. You must believe and demonstrate that the Word of God is the final authority and that you're held captive to what it says. It is authoritative and sufficient for you.
2. Scripture is essential and sufficient for them. Transformation into the image of Christ can't occur without the cleansing and re-creative work of the Word.

Sufficiency: "As much as is needed; equal to what is required; enough, competent."
Authority: "The power or right to give commands, enforce obedience, take action, or make final decisions." *(Webster's Dictionary)*

There are two approaches to demonstrating the authority and sufficiency of Scripture. One is to defend it, debate it, and present an apologetic for its truth. The other is to use it, demonstrating its power firsthand.

Hebrews 4:12 says, "For the word of God is living and active. Sharper than any double-edged sword, it penetrates even to dividing soul and spirit, joints and marrow; it judges the thoughts and attitudes of the heart." You can either debate the power of a sword or use it. But it's far more convincing to simply use a sword than to explain the superior molecular structure of steel. With so many resources today, it is easy to deal with life issues by turning to what other people say rather than what the Scriptures say. New believers need to know that they can go to Scripture, with the power of the Holy Spirit, and hear God speak directly to them. They need to see the Bible as God's love letter to them.

They need to develop the confidence that the Bible speaks today, that it speaks to them and that they can understand it.

1. From these verses, what are some symbols that the Scriptures use to describe itself? Explain the implications.
   Psalm 119:105

   Hebrews 4:12

   James 1:23-25

2. How did Jesus Himself view the Bible?
   Matthew 4:3-11

   Matthew 5:17-20

   Mark 2:24-26

John 8:55-56

John 10:34-35

ROOTING YOURSELF IN GOD'S WORD

As a discipler of others, a key issue is not only the Scriptures' authority but also its sufficiency.

THE WORD AS A KEY TO STABILITY

3. Read Psalm 1:1-3 and draw a picture of what is described.

4. Look at your picture and answer these questions:

What is the tree?

What are the roots?

What is the water?

What is seen/unseen?

How does this compare to spiritual life?

How is a person who meditates on Scripture like a tree?

THE WORD AS POWER FOR VICTORY

5a. What observations can you make regarding the authority and sufficiency of Scripture as Christ faces off with Satan in Matthew 4:1-11?

5b. What are the implications for discipling others?

THE WORD AS ESSENTIAL FOR LIFE

The book of Deuteronomy is a collection of speeches Moses gave at the end of his leadership tenure with Israel. These speeches were a summary of lessons learned from the rocky (and sandy) forty-year period of desert wandering.

As Moses spoke, the people would have been reflecting back on:

- How seventy people came to Egypt some four hundred years earlier and now they numbered in the hundreds of thousands
- How they traded slavery for freedom to claim the Promised Land
- How the Law was given at Mount Sinai
- How the tabernacle and worship were established
- How they failed to believe God at Kadesh Barnea
- How God disciplined Moses for his lack of faith
- How once again they were on the threshold of entering the Promised Land and being honored with a fresh start

6a. Deuteronomy 32:44-47 is a summary of the summary. They are Moses' final words. Read the verses carefully and note:
What is he telling the people to do?

Why is he telling them this?

6b. Paraphrase in your own words this final summary.

The Word as the Key to Prosperity and Success

When Moses dies, he leaves Joshua in charge. Joshua now faces the greatest challenge of his life—to accomplish what even Moses was unable to do. His mission is to lead this nomadic, rebellious, independent, and unpredictable people into the unknown. He was to lead them into the land that their parents had been afraid to invade forty years earlier.

As Joshua steps into the rather large shoes of Moses at this critical point, God speaks to him with the words from Joshua 1:1-9.

7a. In this passage, what promises did God make to Joshua?

7b. What were the conditions for the promises?

7c. What were Joshua's instructions? What was he to do?

7d. What common threads do you see between Joshua 1:1-9 and Deuteronomy 32:45-47?

7e. What are the implications for your life?

ROOTING OTHERS IN GOD'S WORD

As a discipler of others, passing on the belief in the authority and sufficiency of the Bible is of critical importance. As you think of your ministry of disciplemaking, are you confident and dependent on the Word for bringing about change in the lives of others? Do you believe that Scripture is powerful to change lives from the inside out? Do you answer questions, deal with issues, or teach principles from the foundation of Scripture or from logic, experience, and the opinion of others? Are you teaching others to feed themselves from the Scriptures or do they depend on your predigested food?

THE WORD—SKILLED WORKMEN NEEDED

8. Consider 2 Timothy 2:15 and describe in your own words what a workman who correctly handles the Word of Truth would look like.

THE WORD—COMPREHENSIVE EQUIPMENT FOR MINISTRY

9. Read 2 Timothy 3:14-17 and 2 Timothy 4:1-2. Define key words in these passages and summarize what Paul expected from Timothy.

THE WORD FOR A NEW DISCIPLE'S WISDOM

We fail in our duty to study God's Word not so much because it is difficult to understand, not so much because it is dull and boring, but because it is work. Our problem is not a lack of intelligence or lack of passion. Our problem is that we are lazy.

R. C. SPROUL

10a. Read Proverbs 2:1-11. In this passage, what action is required of the "son"?

10b. What promises does the Lord make?

10c. Contrast and compare a search for hidden treasure with gaining life-changing truth from Scripture.

SUMMARY

11. Reflect on these questions:

- Are you modeling the reality that you want to pass on to others?
- The issue isn't so much do you believe the Bible to be true, but does it "hold you captive"?
- When the Bible speaks, do you debate, rationalize, or ignore its teaching?
- Do you know how to dig for Scripture's truth, mine for its gold, and search for its treasure?
- Does it energize you and sustain you?
- Is it your road map, your life manual, your daily source of essential food?
- Is it your protection and sword?
- Are you skilled and confident in your ability to handle it for your life?

12. Drawing from what you've studied, write a statement regarding the authority and sufficiency of Scripture.

13. List ways you can help a disciple come to appreciate and acknowledge the authority and sufficiency of God's Word.

Speaking God's Language

by Joni Eareckson Tada

THE LARGE WINDOW AT Baltimore-Washington International Airport framed a gray afternoon. Our flight was late, and the seats in the waiting area were full. Judy and Bunny stood beside me to pray—something we often do before and after flights.

I was down about a number of things, including the news that we lacked funds to launch an outreach to disabled children in several Eastern European orphanages. Reading the sadness in my eyes, Bunny reached for my hands and Judy's. After praise and thanksgiving, she prayed in a soft voice laced with confidence: "Lord, send forth the corn and the wine and the oil. Send forth the early rains . . . the late rains . . . and produce a wonderful crop of blessings." I recognized the strains of Joel 2:19: "The Lord will reply to them: 'I am sending you grain, new wine and oil, enough to satisfy you fully.'"

Just as Bunny was repeating the part about corn, oil, and wine, I sensed the presence of a fourth person who edged between Judy and me. Then a fifth person crowded in with us, and together the newcomers punctuated my friend's prayer with "amens."

When we finished, we hardly had time to exchange names with our unexpected prayer partners—a married couple. Before rushing to catch their flight, the husband folded a hundred-dollar bill into Bunny's hand. Bunny waved the bill in the air like a flag of victory. "Yes, even while I was speaking in prayer, the angel came with the answer!"

"Joni," she continued as she tucked the bill in my coat pocket, "this is the first-fruits of what God will supply!"

She was right. And it didn't surprise me. When Bunny prays, things happen. I've learned, through years of interceding with her, that Bunny's prayers have power with God.

GOD'S ACCENT

I believe that Bunny's effectiveness in prayer is, at least in part, because she has learned to pray in the language of the Father. Bunny even responds using God's language: Her "even while I was speaking in prayer" was a paraphrase of Daniel 9:21.

I've learned to follow Bunny's lead and season my prayers with the Word of God. It's a way of talking to God in His language—speaking His dialect, using His vernacular, employing His idioms. (I've often teased Bunny that I hear God's accent when she prays.)

If praying "in the name of Jesus" comes as naturally as breathing, we need to pray "in the Word" just as naturally. The Bible underscores God honors two things above all else: His name and His Word. "For you have exalted above all things your name and your word," wrote David in Psalm 138:2. Prayer spiced with God's Word is prayer exalted.

This isn't simply a matter of divine vocabulary. It's a matter of power. When we bring God's Word directly into our praying, we're bringing God's power into our praying. Hebrews 4:12 declares, "For the word of God is living and active. Sharper than any double-edged sword." God's Word is living, and so it infuses our prayers with life and vitality. God's Word is also active, injecting energy and power into our prayers. Listen to how God described His words to Jeremiah: "Is not my word like fire . . . and like a hammer that breaks a rock in pieces?" (Jeremiah 23:29). Scripture gives muscle and might to our prayers.

YOUR PRAYER BOOK

I'm convinced that God enjoys it when we consciously employ His Word in our prayers. It shows Him the importance we attach to our requests. It demonstrates that we've thought through our petitions and praises and lined them up against the plumb line of Scripture. It underscores to Him the high regard and appreciation we attach to His Word and demonstrates that we sincerely seek His heart in the matter we're praying for. Using God's Word in prayer—Scripture praying, as it is sometimes called—gives a divine familiarity to our words, earmarking us as servants who possess a working knowledge of the most powerful prayer book ever written: the Bible.

Saints in Scripture practiced this type of praying. The prophet Habakkuk appealed to God on the basis of His Word during a time of deep national distress: The ruthless Babylonian army was poised to sweep across the country like water from a ruptured dam. Yes, the prophet agreed with the Lord that Judah was deserving of His judgment. But how could God use a people even more evil than they as His rod of discipline? Habakkuk quoted snippets of Psalms and Proverbs as he spoke with God: "Your eyes are too pure to look on evil; you cannot tolerate wrong. Why then do you tolerate the treacherous? Why are you silent while the wicked swallow up those more righteous than themselves?" (Habakkuk 1:13).

David pleaded with God in prayer based on what he knew to be true about the Lord from Scripture: "Remember, O Lord, your great mercy and love, for they are from of old . . . According to your love remember me, for you are good, O Lord" (Psalm 25:6-7).

Does it sound cheeky to remind God of His character and His promises? Does it seem presumptuous? Perhaps, if you're unfamiliar with the prayer habits of saints such as Habakkuk and David. Still, the Lord would have us claim His love, plead His holiness, remind Him of His goodness, recount His longsuffering, present to Him His steadfastness, and pray in His power. In Isaiah 1:18, God invites us: "Come now, let us reason together." He encourages our discourse.

WORD-WOVEN PRAYERS

I often attend prayer meetings where various requests for healing, finances, safety in travel, or job promotions are divvied out. Naturally, we desire prayer for such things. But a closer look at God's Word reveals deeper and more divinely inspired ways to pray for friends and family.

Is there a cancer? Yes, prayer for healing is in order, but so is prayer for the robust blessings of Psalm 119:140: "Your promises have been thoroughly tested, and your servant loves them." How rich to pray, "Lord, this cancer is testing Your promises in the life of my friend who is ill, but You are faithful to every promise You've made to her. May Your servant love Your promises through this time of testing."

Is there a need for finances? Yes, prayer for needed money is in order, but so is prayer for the rewards of Proverbs 15:17: "Better a meal of vegetables where there is love than a fattened calf with hatred." How invigorating to pray, "Lord, financial blessing isn't the focus; Your Word says that love should be. May we learn to live on little if it means leaning harder on You as well as each other."

When I pray for disabled children I know, I intercede with Matthew 19:14 in mind: "Jesus said, 'Let the little children come to me, and do not hinder them, for the kingdom of heaven belongs to such as these.'" In Matthew 19:15 we're given a picture of Jesus tenderly placing His hand on each child. "Lord Jesus," I'll say, "Your heart went out to children when You walked on earth. I can picture You tousling their hair, bouncing them on Your knee, and laying Your hands on their heads to bestow a blessing. If Your heart went out this way to the boys and girls who could walk up to You, how much more must Your heart overflow toward little Jeanette with spina bifida or Benjamin who has cerebral palsy. Today, may they feel Your hand of blessing on their heads."

Often, it's appropriate to quote an entire passage, substituting a person's name for the pronoun in the passage. Colossians 1:9-12 is a good example of Scripture to pray this way: "I ask God to fill Susan with the knowledge of His will through all spiritual wisdom and understanding. And I pray this in order that Susan may live a life worthy of the Lord and may please Him in every way: bearing fruit in every good work she does, being strengthened with all power, so that she may have great endurance and patience, and joyfully give thanks to the Father."

Remember, God's Word is alive, active, and powerful. Prayers laced with the Word of God not only bring about fundamental changes in people and situations, but such prayers keep us in touch with God's priorities. Weaving God's Word into our prayers brings His purposes to the forefront of every request.

LANGUAGE LESSONS

Bunny is a good instructor on how to pray using Scripture. She'd suggest that, first, we must read long portions of God's Word, not necessarily as Bible study, but to seek insights that we might apply to petitions or praises. Next, we should meditate on those portions that reveal a particular truth we can apply in prayer. Evaluate how a passage might translate into a specific petition, asking yourself, "Does this verse prompt me to pray for someone with such a need? Is it possible to use some of the words of this Scripture as I pray?" Then form a personal prayer, enriched by the passage you've chosen.

As you center your prayers on God's Word, its power and life become not only a part of those for whom you pray but also a part of you. Focus on quoting God's mercies in prayer as David did, and you'll become more merciful. Plead with Him for His wisdom, quoting Proverbs 4, and wisdom will be yours. Center your requests upon His holiness, and you'll grow in holiness.

AN ENLARGEMENT OF HIS PROMISES

E. M. Bounds was known for his extraordinary prayer life. He once testified,

> The Word of God is the fulcrum upon which the lever of prayer is placed, and by which things are mightily moved. God has committed Himself, His purpose, and His promise to prayer. His Word becomes the basis, the inspiration of our praying, and there are circumstances under which by importunate prayer, we may obtain an . . . enlargement of His promises.

Bunny would say, "Amen!" I would, too. I will never forget the time I received an "enlargement of His promises" from praying Scripture. It was in the early 1980s, not long after the honeymoon was over for two newlyweds: Ken and me. I learned that my new husband preferred to spend Monday nights in front of the TV with chips, salsa, and the NFL rather than being my hands to write out my Bible study for me. Horrors, I thought—he's not a man of the Word!

I was itching to change my husband, but my nagging and scolding only made things worse. Feeling like a martyr, I sought help in God's Word and stumbled across these words in Philippians 2:3-4: "Do nothing out of selfish ambition or vain conceit, but in humility consider others better than yourselves. Each of you should look not only to your own interests, but also to the interests of others."

Yikes, that's me, I thought. I've wanted Ken to change for selfish reasons—so that he'll meet my expectations. And to be honest, I don't consider him "better than myself." I feel I'm the one in the right. I feel I've got it spiritually together, not him.

Convicted. These verses catapulted me into a major prayer advance for Ken. I sincerely wanted to follow God's Word and have humility of mind, as well as to regard Ken as better than I. How could I look out for his interests? I feverishly flipped through Scripture until I found the perfect passage to pray for my husband.

Who may ascend the hill of the Lord? Who may stand in his holy place? He who has clean hands and a pure heart, who does not lift up his soul to an idol or swear by what is false. He will receive blessing from the Lord and vindication from God his Savior. Such is the generation of those who seek him, who seek your face, O God of Jacob. Selah. Lift up your heads, O you gates; be lifted up, you ancient doors, that the King of glory may come in. Who is this King of glory? The Lord strong and mighty, the Lord mighty in battle. (Psalm 24:3-8)

I'd spend evenings in our bedroom, praying, "Lord, You want Ken to stand in Your holy place, to have clean hands and a pure heart. May You cause him to lift up his soul to You and receive Your blessing. May he seek Your face. Lift up the gates of Ken's heart that You, the King of glory, might come in! Lord, say to him, 'I, the King of glory, will come in and rule your life. I, the Lord, strong and mighty.'"

I can't tell you how many times I prayed this way. But now, years later, it's clear that Christ sits on the throne of my husband's heart. (He's in the process of memorizing the entire Sermon on the Mount; I didn't put him up to it—really!) Something else is clear: Ken still loves Monday Night Football. What has changed is that so do I! And I've found other "hands" to help me write out my Bible studies on other evenings.

I began praying Psalm 24 over my husband, believing that God would change him, but God did much more. He changed me. It was, as E. M. Bounds would say, "an enlargement of His promises." I'm convinced that we're still feeling the repercussions of that Scripture prayer. That's because it was based on Psalm 24 and was alive, active, and powerful, bringing about fundamental changes in me where it counted most. And in my husband, too.

The Bible is our prayer book, and we'd be remiss to neglect its riches. It holds the key to finding God's will when we pray, providing balance and meaning. Great themes abound— God's holiness, wisdom, faithfulness, sovereignty, love, and mercy—all of which beautify our praises, adorn our intercessions, embroider our petitions, and give weight and significance to every supplication.

Most of all, using the Word of God in prayer is about as close as we can get to the Living Word, the Lord Jesus. If we're going to pray in His name, it makes sense to speak in His language.[1]

———◆———

ABOUT THE AUTHOR: Joni Eareckson Tada is president of JAF Ministries, an organization that accelerates Christian ministry into the disabled community around the world. She is also author of several books, including *When God Weeps* and *More Precious Than Silver* (both published by Zondervan).

QUESTIONS FOR REFLECTION

1. Why is praying Scripture beneficial? (Include your own thoughts as well as insight from the article.)
2. How could you make praying Scripture more of a practice in your own life?

▶ TIPS FOR DISCIPLING

How to Pray for Your Disciple Using the Scriptures
by John D. Purvis

What follows are some lessons my wife and I have learned in praying for others; especially using the power of the Bible. We know we're safe if we're appealing to God based on what He's already said about a challenge or an issue in a new disciple's life.

A. USE A CONCORDANCE OR BIBLE COMPUTER PROGRAM TO LOOK UP SCRIPTURES

Let's say my disciple has difficulty with harsh speech. I go to my Bible concordance and look up the topic. I may find corollary words such as *speak, tongue, words*. I find verses that show a promise, a plea, or a principle. I put the verses I like into my prayer pages for the disciple.

B. PRAY THESE SCRIPTURES FOR A NEW DISCIPLE

Example: Asking God to mellow Jake's harsh speech:

- *Proverbs 21:23—"He who guards his mouth and his tongue keeps himself from calamity."*
- *Proverbs 25:15—"Through patience a ruler can be persuaded, and a gentle tongue can break a bone."*
- *Ephesians 4:29—"Do not let any unwholesome talk come out of your mouths, but only what is helpful for building others up according to their needs, that it may benefit those who listen."*
- *Colossians 4:6—Let your conversation be always full of grace, seasoned with salt, so that*

you may know how to answer everyone."

- *James 3:9-10—"With the tongue we praise ourLord and Father, and with it we curse men, who have been made in God's likeness. Out of the same mouth come praise and cursing. My brothers, this should not be."*

That [NAME] would pray about everything and be thankful under all circumstances:

- Philippians 4:6
- 1 Thessalonians 5:18

That [NAME] would see wonderful things as he/she reads God's Word:

- Psalm 119:18

That [NAME] would grow in his/her understanding of who Jesus is:

- Colossians 1:15-17

That [NAME] would be rooted and built up in Christ, strengthened in his/her faith and thankful:

- Colossians 2:6-7

That the blood of the Lamb would break Satan's stronghold on [NAME's] life:

- 1 Peter 1:18-19

That [NAME] would bear fruit that would last and see God answer his/her prayers:

- John 15:16

That [NAME] would consider everything a loss compared to knowing Christ:

- Philippians 3:7-8

That [NAME] would seek God with his/her whole heart:

- Deuteronomy 4:29
- Jeremiah 24:6-7

That [NAME] would reflect the glory of Christ to a world that desperately needs to see a clearer view of who God really is:

- 2 Corinthians 3:18

• 2 Corinthians 5:15

C. PRAYING POSITIVELY INTO PEOPLE'S LIVES INSTEAD OF COMPLAINING

Using the following chart, pray that God will bless him or her with the positive when we are aware of the negative.

What qualities we see negatively	What we can thank God for positively	What qualities we see negatively	What we can thank God for positively
Blunt, outspoken	Honesty	Money squanderer, wasteful	Generosity
Cliquish, social climber	Hospitality	Nonchalant, indifferent	Patient
Competitive, over-ambition	Aspiration	Nosy	Inquisitive
Compromising, conniving	Cooperative	Nervous	Alert
Conceited, proud	Confident	No convictions	Amiable
Crabby, picky	Detailed	One-track mind	Diligence
Dependency, subservient	Respectful	Opinionated	Strong convictions
Distractible	Spontaneous	Over-attention to detail	Analytical
Domineering	Leadership	Overbearing	Enthusiasm
Flatterer	Gratefulness	Overzealous, fanatical	Sincere
Harsh, overbearing	Truthful	Perfectionist	Neat
Holier-than-thou, self-righteous	Spiritual	Possessive	Loyalty
Impatient	Efficiency	Pushy, smooth-tongued	Persuasive
Independent	Resoluteness	Reckless, brash	Courage
Indecisive, wishy-washy	Flexibility	Rigid, tyrannical	Discipline
Inferiority	Meekness	Secretive	Loyal
Inflexible	Decisive	Self-willed, inflexible	Persistence

chart continued on next page

What qualities we see negatively	What we can thank God for positively	What qualities we see negatively	What we can thank God for positively
Insensitive, unloving	Objectivity	Sentimental, gushy	Compassion
Insulting, tactless	Frankness	Serious	Earnestness
Intense	Focused	Stingy, miserly, tightwad	Frugal
Irresponsible		Stubborn, hard-headed, inflexible	Determined
Judgmental	Fair-minded	Superiority, sophistication	Positive
Lazy		Talkative, chatterbox	Expressive
Legalist	Respect rules	Tight-fisted	Frugal
Low self-esteem, self abasement	Humility	Timid, cautious, careful	Discretion
Manipulative, scheming	Planner	Touchy, easily offended	Sensitive
Meticulous, scrupulous	Specialist	Weak, condoning	Forgiving
Mischievous, crafty	Creative		

THE VALUE OF EACH INDIVIDUAL

LESSON PLAN

- Share highlights from personal devotional times.
- Review Isaiah 60:22.
- Discuss "The Value of Each Individual" Bible study.
- Discuss the article "The Importance of Every Individual."
- Using a passage or principle from the study and article, pray for those you are discipling.
- Share what obstacles and challenges those you're discipling may still need to face.
- Discuss Tips for Discipling: "Don't Give Up Yet."

ASSIGNMENT FOR SESSION 12: SPIRITUAL GENERATIONS

- Prepare "Spiritual Generations" Bible study.
- Memorize 2 Timothy 2:1-2.
- Review Scripture memory.
- Read "Motivation: For a Lifetime of Disciplemaking."
- Continue personal devotional times.
- Read Tips for Discipling: "Discipling over the Long Haul."
- Continue to meet with your growing disciples.

GROUP PRAYER REQUESTS

▶ BIBLE STUDY

THE VALUE OF EACH INDIVIDUAL

KEY ISSUES

- How do we see the value of each individual?
- What impact can a few have upon society and eventually the world?
- What is our commitment to invest in others?

Currently, six-billion-plus people live on this planet. So how important is one? When you're part of a group of five and one doesn't show up, the absence is obvious. You miss that person. But what about one person in a church of five hundred? Or one person in a city of four million? How valuable is one person to God out of the billions now on this planet? How about one person from all the people who have ever lived?

God's view is often very different from ours. God sees not only masses but also individuals. He sees not only the popular but also the obscure. He sees not only the talented but also the simple. God's purposes are also often different from our purposes. God tends to pick the little people, the average garden-variety type rather than the tall, stately, highly intelligent, and the ones born with a golden spoon in their mouths. Isaiah 60:21-22 has this to say about the high potential of an individual: "Then will all your people be righteous and they will possess the land forever. They are the shoot I have planted, the work of my hands, for the display of my splendor. The least of you will become a thousand, the smallest a mighty nation. I am the LORD; in its time I will do this swiftly."

PEOPLE HAVE INTRINSIC VALUE

It can be tempting to value people in terms of what they can do for us, or how they can benefit something in our worlds. However, God says,

> The LORD did not set his affection on you and choose you because you were more
> numerous than other peoples, for you were the fewest of all peoples. But it was
> because the LORD loved you and kept the oath he swore to your forefathers that he
> brought you out with a mighty hand and redeemed you from the land of slavery, from

the power of Pharaoh king of Egypt. Know therefore that the LORD your God is God; he is the faithful God, keeping his covenant of love to a thousand generations of those who love him and keep his commands. (Deuteronomy 7:7-9)

I (John) can remember—as a young believer—a man whose life ate and breathed evangelism. I questioned him about his intense heart for people. He told me that for two years as a Christian he was literally frozen into silence when trying to tell someone else about Jesus Christ. Then he had a life-changing thought. He decided to view everyone he met by imagining them as the next Billy Graham, or the next Mother Teresa. After that, it was not difficult for him to talk to people. And indeed, he has influenced some people who have become big influencers in God's kingdom.

GOD'S HEART FOR PEOPLE

No theme is more pronounced throughout the pages of Scripture than the heart of God for people.

1. Look at the following sample verses and note what place people have with God.
   Psalm 8:3-8

   Psalm 116:15

   Isaiah 43:4

   2 Peter 3:9

GOD IS RELATIONAL

God not only relates to groups of people, nations, and clans, but also to individuals. God not only has a heart for people, but for persons. Scripture reveals a God who longs to relate to each person individually. Genealogies in the Old Testament, though boring for most of us, show God's relationship with individual people.

2a. How do the following verses demonstrate God's involvement with individual people?
   2 Chronicles 16:9

Jeremiah 32:19

Ezekiel 22:30

Hebrews 4:13

2b. God is intimately familiar with each one of us. How is God's intimate knowledge of each person demonstrated in the following verses?
1 Samuel 16:7

2 Chronicles 16:9

Psalm 139:1-6

Psalm 139:13-18

Ephesians 2:8-10

2c. How should God's involvement with individual people affect our attitudes and behavior?

THE IMPACT OF ORDINARY LIVES

There are no ordinary people.[1]

C. S. Lewis

God not only relates to us as individuals, but also sees the potential and significance of each individual. The value of a person within God's purposes is impossible to comprehend. But, it's huge.

3a. Reflecting on your knowledge of individual Bible characters, highlight the contribution and influence each person had on his or her world. How was each person "ordinary"? Select at least two of the illustrations below and answer the following two questions: (1) What did they contribute or what kind of impact did they have? and (2) How were they ordinary?

Noah (Genesis 6–10)

Joseph (Genesis 37–47)

Rahab (Joshua 2; 6:23; Matthew 1:5; Hebrews 11:31)

Barnabas (Acts 4:36; 9:27; 11:22-30; 13)

Lydia (Acts 16:11-40)

3b. Scripture often surprises us with God's use of the common person. How do these verses illustrate the value of each person?

1 Corinthians 1:26-29

1 Corinthians 12:14-26

2 Corinthians 4:7

2 Timothy 2:20-21

1 Peter 2:5

3c. What examples from your own experience demonstrate your value as an ordinary person?

JESUS MODELS THE WORTH OF THE INDIVIDUAL

4. Using the following chart, reflect on the lives of the individuals Jesus touched.

Person	How did Jesus demonstrate the worth of the individual?	What resulted from His personal attention?
Demoniac (Mark 5:1-20)		
Zacchaeus (Luke 19:1-10)		
Woman at well (John 4:3-30, 39-42)		

SUMMARY

5. What is one key idea has God has impressed upon you from this study?

6. How can you apply what you've learned from this study?

The Importance of Every Individual

by Lorne Sanny

IMAGINE FOR A MOMENT that you own a valuable treasure. You would, of course, value it highly. And suppose that obtaining this treasure had cost you very dearly. You'd cherish it all the more. And suppose you knew that in the future your treasure would become even greater in its beauty and worth. You would, if possible, consider it more precious still. *You* are all this, and more, to God.

Let's think a moment, about you.

The Bible admonishes each of us, "Do not think of yourself more highly than you ought, but rather think of yourself with sober judgment, in accordance with the measure of faith God has given you" (Romans 12:3). Discussing the importance of every individual—your importance—is necessary because many of us just don't think with sober judgment about ourselves. It seems we fluctuate from one extreme to another.

I heard about a man who went to a psychiatrist and complained that his friends were all avoiding him. The psychiatrist asked him to sit down and tell him everything, starting at the beginning.

"Alright," the man said. "In the beginning, I created the heavens and the earth."

That's just a story, but there are some Christians who are like the cat who frequently had its tail stepped on. Its self-image was so low that the cat resigned itself to a lifetime of having its tail stepped on. Whenever someone came by, it simply turned and stuck out its tail. Many of us may, deep in our hearts, feel just that way.

How about you? Maybe you feel uncomfortable down inside, insecure or fearful or frustrated. You smile as you pass by others and you laugh with your friends, but you know the truth of Proverbs 14:13: "Even in laughter the heart may ache, and joy may end in grief." Have you ever put a smile on your face to hide a tear in your heart? Sometimes, as you know, outward bravado simply masks inner insecurity.

Why do we have these attitudes toward ourselves? One reason is that we compare ourselves with others. The Bible says this is unwise. The result is invariably bad: Either we think we're better than someone else, so we become proud; or we think we're worse and become depressed.

We also look at ourselves and others from a mere human point of view. Yet we read in 2 Corinthians 5:16, "From now on we regard no one from a human point of view." In this chapter, Paul was explaining what it means to be a new creation in Christ. He said he once regarded even Christ from a human point of view, but no longer. Now we also can see Christ, as well as each other and ourselves, from God's point of view.

God is interested in individuals. I like Jesus' parable in Luke 15 of the ninety-nine sheep and the one that was lost. The shepherd left the ninety-nine and went out until he found the missing one. Jesus was telling us of the importance God places on one person.

At another time, Jesus was coming into Jericho. The streets were jammed with people so a short man named Zacchaeus climbed a tree to see him. When Jesus came by, of all the people there, he picked out this one little guy and said, "Come down, Zacchaeus, I'm coming to your house today!"

And when Lazarus, the brother of Mary and Martha, had died in Bethany, Jesus went there. After Martha had spoken with Jesus, she went to Mary and said, "The Teacher is here and is asking for you." That is true also for us. The Lord is here and he's calling for you. It's not like seeing someone beckon in your direction, and then discovering it's for someone else. No, the Lord asks for you, because you're important to him.

I can give you three reasons why you're important to God: (1) simply because of who you are; (2) because of what you cost; and (3) because of what you can become.

YOU'RE CREATED IN THE IMAGE OF GOD

"God said, 'Let us make man in our image, in our Likeness . . .' So God created man in his own image, in the image of God he created him; male and female he created them" (Genesis 1:26-27).

People often ask, "Who am I?" I've come to see that this question is impossible to answer without mentioning a relationship to someone else. And the ultimate answer is who I am in relationship to God.

Who are you? You're a being created in God's image. That means first that you have a unique, recognizable personality.

Not only are you an original personality, but God gave you the power of abstract thought. You can ask such questions as "Who am I?" or "Why am I here?" and "Where am I going?"

You also have a moral faculty. You can choose right or wrong. In fact, the concept of right and wrong is built into you. The Ten Commandments are the expression of God's character, and they're written into the laws of the universe and into the constitution of every human being. That's made evident by the fact that people aren't content just to sin, but they have to justify it. They may go to great lengths to justify their sins, because a moral law exists within them.

One of my children, before he was five, was sitting next to me on the couch and looked up and asked me this blockbuster: "Daddy, what makes me naughty?" Not yet five, but he knew right from wrong. God has built that into every human being.

Not only do you have personality, the power of abstract thought, and a moral faculty, but you also have a spiritual nature. Something inside us makes us feel empty and unsatisfied until we experience God. We're restless until we discover what's beyond us. Ecclesiastes 3:11 says that God "set eternity in the hearts of men." Something inside tells us we were made for eternity. A flower blooms and dies; but a person continues forever to be, to think, to feel.

You're valuable. In fact, one individual is worth more than the whole earth. Jesus said, "What good is it for a man to gain the whole world, yet forfeit his soul? Or what can a man give in exchange for his soul?" (Mark 8:36-37).

YOU'RE IMPORTANT BECAUSE OF WHAT YOU COST

On a visit to Hawaii, we saw quilts for sale for $800. We asked why they cost so much and were told that they were handmade by South Sea islanders who spent seven to eight months making each one. Those quilts cost hundreds of working hours to make—and the value of something is determined by its cost.

Now think of what you cost God: "God so loved the world [you!] that he gave his one and only Son." You cost God the best heaven had.

When I was with the Billy Graham team at a crusade in Scotland, one of the reporters covering the meetings was back at his newspaper office where other staff members were criticizing the crusade. This reporter found himself defending Billy Graham. "Why, Billy Graham preaches that Christ died for sinners," he said, warming to his subject. "In fact," he said, "Christ died for me." In that instant, he suddenly realized for the first time that Christ had indeed died for him; he believed and was born again.

Have you seen Christ on the cross for you? That's what you cost God, and you are valuable to God by virtue of that cost. Peter wrote, "It was not with perishable things such as silver or gold that you were redeemed from the empty way of life handed down to you from your forefathers, but with the precious blood of Christ, a lamb without blemish or defect" (1 Peter 1:18-19).

Don't ever say you or anyone else is worthless. That's a human point of view. A person may be lazy, or dull, or aggravating, or even repulsive, but he's not worthless. He was created in the image of God, and he was purchased by the blood of Christ.

YOU'RE IMPORTANT BECAUSE OF WHAT YOU CAN BECOME

This occurs under the transforming power of the Holy Spirit. Another of my favorite verses is John 1:42: "Then he brought Simon to Jesus, who looked at him and said, 'You are Simon son of John. You will be called Cephas (which, when translated, is Peter)." Jesus looked at Simon and said, "You are . . . but you will be . . ."

Jesus saw in Simon what he could become under the Holy Spirit's power: You are Simon; you will be Peter. You're a small stone; you'll be a big rock. You're a moral coward now; you'll be courageous. You're unreliable and unstable; you'll be stable and steady. We see what Jesus meant when Peter abjectly denied his Lord, but later preached Christ boldly to the leaders in Jerusalem.

You may be filled with hostility, but God can fill you with forgiveness. You may be filled with impure thoughts, but Christ can make your thoughts pure. You may be fearful, but He can fill your life with peace.

A few years ago, I received a letter from a businessman taking me to task for something that

I wasn't actually involved in. I could have written to him explaining that I didn't have a part in this situation. But I prayed about it and instead telephoned him and asked if we could have lunch together. When we did, no sooner had we placed the order than his lip began to quiver.

"Lorne," he said, "I'm sorry I wrote you that letter. I've been filled with hostility for years. My wife and I don't communicate and we haven't for years, I've driven off my children, I have a war on with my neighbors, and it seems I'm constantly at odds with the people I work for. It pervades my whole life. And I just feel if I don't get it straightened out soon this will be my last chance." Then he said, "I need a parole officer, someone I need to check in with."

"If you would like, I'll be your parole officer," I answered. "You can check in with me." He began coming over to my home, and the first thing I got him to do was to memorize Ephesians 4:30-32: "And grieve not the Holy Spirit of God, whereby ye are sealed unto the day of redemption. Let all bitterness, and wrath, and anger, and clamour, and evil speaking be put away from you, with all malice; and be ye kind one to another, tenderhearted, forgiving one another, even as God for Christ's sake hath forgiven you."

He began to write letters to people he'd offended. He apologized to his children, and made things right with his wife. He and his wife began to communicate, the children began coming home, and even his high blood pressure came down.

Such is the transforming power of the Holy Spirit. You are . . . but you will be . . .

You're important to God the Father because of creation, to God the Son because of redemption, and to God the Holy Spirit because of sanctification. In light of all this, what should we do? Romans 12:1 tells us, "Therefore, I urge you, brothers, in view of God's mercy, to offer your bodies as living sacrifices, holy and pleasing to God—which is your spiritual worship."

Because he created you in his image, because you cost him the blood of his Son, and because his Holy Spirit can powerfully transform you—offer yourself to God.

I once heard a Christian youth leader tell of a conference where everyone gathered around a fireplace at the closing meeting. They were throwing little sticks into the fire as a kind of symbol of what they were committing to the Lord. Then one fellow said, "I'm giving my cigarettes to the Lord," and he tossed in a package of cigarettes. The youth leader quickly got a stick and pulled out the package before it burned.

Handing it back to the fellow, he said, "God doesn't want or need your cigarettes. God wants you."

God wants us to humbly surrender ourselves. I like the hymn "Channels Only." We're not reservoirs, but channels. We're not power plants, but transmission lines. God has the power, God is the reservoir, and we should surrender ourselves to Him so He can work through us.

In the exchange of marriage vows the woman doesn't turn to the man and say, "I give you my cooking ability." Nor does he say to her, "I give you my bank account." No, in a marriage ceremony they vow, "I give you myself." That's what Romans 12:1 is about. It means saying to God, "I give you me."

God has given His best to you. Is your best His? Your best begins with committing yourself totally to Him. Then God will have your feet to take you where He wants you to go. He'll have your ears to listen to those who need listening to. He'll have your mouth to speak what He wants spoken. He'll also have your time, your career, and your money.

Have you ever said a once-for-all yes to the Lord, like the yes one says in a marriage ceremony? Not only that, but as a living sacrifice are you following the big yes with a lot of small ones? I'm convinced this continual surrender is the key to being used by God. That's what it means to take up your cross daily—a once-for-all commitment to follow Jesus Christ as His disciple, followed by a lot of little commitments and adjustments and surrenders along the way.

In giving yourself, you're turning over to God the most valuable thing you can give.[2]

QUESTIONS FOR REFLECTION

1. How do you respond to the author's statement, "Outward bravado simply masks inner insecurity"?
2. Which of the three reasons given for the worth of every individual seems most relevant to those you are discipling? Why?

▶ TIPS FOR DISCIPLING

Don't Give Up Yet

by Kathy Kelly

Discipling fellow believers is often rewarding, but what happens when the one you've invested in so much begins to slip away? It's frustrating and heartbreaking to see those you've discipled fall back into old behaviors or lose their desire for Christian growth. It's also difficult to know what to do next.

Here are some tips for revitalizing a discipling relationship that may be headed for the rocks.

1. DON'T GIVE UP

It can be tempting to wash your hands of the situation and gear your efforts toward another new believer. Remember that God never gives up on you, no matter how far you stray! Although you aren't responsible for another's lagging interest and unwillingness to be discipled, don't stop making the effort to lead this person back to the path of Christian growth.

2. BE PATIENT WITH IMMATURITY

When you first accepted Christ, God didn't deal immediately with every sin in your life. Your life changed gradually and continues to change as you grow closer to the Lord. In discipling new believers, be patient as they struggle with the concept of conforming to the image of Christ.

3. CONFRONT SIN

On the flip side, however, don't hesitate to confront lovingly your disciples when they fall into sin. The truth, gently presented, can help a straying disciple make a fresh commitment to Christ.

4. VARY YOUR METHODS

You may recapture the interest of a struggling believer by occasionally changing your approach. If your pattern is to use your time strictly for Bible study, hold a question-and-answer session instead. Leave the notebooks at home for a change, and go for ice cream and a discussion of personal issues.

5. PRESENT NEW CHALLENGES

It's difficult to know when a believer is ready to take a new step of faith, but a seeming lack of steady progress may indicate it's time for a new challenge. Ask your friend to teach a Sunday school class, lead prayer, or give his testimony at your next small group meeting. Remind him that the added responsibility will require greater commitment.

6. PRAY

Above all else, pray for those you disciple. There's nothing Satan would like more than to see new believers give up and remain ineffective servants of Christ. You can help win the battle for the lives of these struggling believers by fighting on your knees.

Discipling isn't easy, but the rewards of seeing a new believer begin to live a victorious Christian life are priceless. If you're struggling in your discipling relationships, take heart! With prayer, creativity, and perseverance, you may see your straying friend return to the path of righteousness.[3]

SPIRITUAL GENERATIONS

LESSON PLAN

- Share highlights from personal devotional times.
- Review 2 Timothy 2:1-2.
- Discuss the Bible study "Spiritual Generations."
- Share lessons you've learned regarding discipling others life-to-life.
- Discuss "Motivation: For a Lifetime of Disciplemaking."
- Share what progress you've seen in your new disciples over the duration of the course.
- Discuss Tips for Discipling: "Discipling over the Long Haul."

FINAL ASSIGNMENT

- Celebrate. Have a party!
- Decide what happens next. For example, should each person now function as a coach?

GROUP PRAYER REQUESTS

▶ BIBLE STUDY

SPIRITUAL GENERATIONS

KEY ISSUES
- What does "spiritual generations" mean?
- How is the concept of spiritual generations used in Scripture?
- How does fruitfulness and discipling others relate to spiritual generations?

Spiritual generations, multiplication, reproduction, fruitfulness, descendants, offspring, lineage . . . these words are all used in Scripture to convey a concept that runs from Genesis to Revelation. In the following study, we want to look at this concept that's so important to God and see how it can affect our lives.

Generations are built in the very DNA of nature. Every living thing has within it the power to reproduce itself, from the simple single-cell amoeba to the complex human being. We see it every spring as new life buds from the dormant plants. Animals bear their young according to a fixed cycle. Reproduction is essential to our natural world. Should we expect it to be any different in the spiritual world?

God's passion is to bring blessing to the nations through Jesus. Jesus Himself said He came to seek and to save that which was lost. The Father desires that our lives and ministries be fruitful and that our fruit multiply to many generations. Fruitfulness is rooted in God's blessing of mankind. The gospel is a generational trust, a legacy passed through descendants. The pursuit of passing on the gospel to the next generation is at the very heart of the Great Commission.

General Definitions
- *Generation*—the process of producing offspring, a single stage in the succession of natural descent
- *Multiply*—to cause to increase in number
- *Reproduce*—to make a copy, duplicate; to produce by propagation, bring forth

Working Definitions
- *Spiritual reproduction*—the concept that God works through believers to bring forth new spiritual life in others

- *Spiritual generations*—the concept that every believer should be involved in bringing forth a new generation of believers
- *Spiritual multiplication*—the concept of spiritual reproduction working over time and through successive spiritual generations

1. What do the following verses contribute to the concept of spiritual generations?
   Genesis 17:7-10

   Deuteronomy 6:4-9

   Psalm 103:17-18

   Isaiah 44:3

FOUNDATION OF GENERATIONS

Reproduction in nature is so axiomatic that we rarely stop to question or wonder at it. Medical scientists have utilized this power for health advancements, and agricultural researchers have tapped it for greater food production. But how have we captured it in building God's kingdom?

2a. "Be fruitful and multiply" is repeated throughout the book of Genesis. Look at these references and note the results that come from this command.
   Genesis 1:22

   Genesis 8:17

   Genesis 9:1

   Genesis 35:11

The apostle Paul frequently used a family metaphor in his letters to illustrate the new relationships we have as followers of Christ. In Romans 4, Paul positions Abraham, who was considered the patriarch of the Jewish race, as father of the family of faith.

This new faith family consists of those who, like Abraham, believe the promises of God. This new lineage is made up of spiritual generations—parents and children. As part of that spiritual heritage, Paul then refers to those who believed God's promise through his ministry as his children.

- Galatians 4:19: "My dear children, for whom I am again in the pains of childbirth until Christ is formed in you . . ."
- 1 Timothy 1:2: "To Timothy my true son in the faith . . ."

Abraham's big family is a spiritual one—a family of faith. It expands throughout history one generation—one person—at a time. It involves fathers and mothers, sisters and brothers. Unfortunately, this family model, with spiritual parents and children, with generational responsibility and loving care, has largely been replaced with a Christian orphanage model, one with a lot of children but few parents—children trying to grow up by watching their peers rather than under the guidance of a spiritual parent.

2b. Look at some generational passages from the New Testament. What generational issues are involved in these verses?
John 17:20

Romans 4:16-18

Galatians 3:7-9

Hebrews 11:12

Revelation 7:9

2c. Summarize your key observations about the role of generations in building God's kingdom.

GENERATIONS AND FRUITFULNESS

Much of Jesus' teaching about fruitfulness and spiritual generations comes from examples in nature.

3a. What do these passages teach about fruitfulness?
   Matthew 13:18-23

   John 12:24-25

   John 15:1-16

3b. How do these principles relate to spiritual multiplication?

The test of any work of evangelism is not what is seen at the moment but in the effectiveness with which the work continues into the next generation.

ROBERT COLEMAN

MULTIPLE GENERATIONS

The Scripture often refers to multiple generations. God seems to place great value on successive generations following Him. His design is for each generation to pass on a spiritual dynamic to the next generation.

4a. Identify the generations referred to in the following passages.

Example: Job 42:16-17
   Job, sons, grandsons, fourth generation

Deuteronomy 6:4-9

Deuteronomy 32:45-46

Psalm 78:1-4

Psalm 145:4-5

Isaiah 59:21

Joel 1:1-3

Matthew 28:19-20

2 Timothy 2:2

1 Thessalonians 1:5-9

4b. In 1 Corinthians 4:14-17, Paul sees himself as a father/mother rather than an instructor in his ministry to the new believers in Corinth. Why? What is the benefit?

The first time I met Craig, he was a student at Mankato State University. He was fun-loving, had a great laugh and sense of humor, and was well liked on campus. But there was much more to his story . . . Years earlier, a man by the name of Mike had helped Randy begin a personal relationship with Jesus Christ. Randy, in faithfulness to God, passed on the gospel message to a young man named Craig Meyer.

Craig, a Minnesota farm kid, was in college now because he wanted to make his life count for God. During the first few weeks of school, Craig befriended Jeff. They developed a good friendship and, as Mike had done with Randy, and as Randy had done with Craig, Craig shared about his spiritual journey with Jeff. Jeff, too, embraced the gospel of Jesus Christ and gave his heart to Him. Craig influenced others like Hua, Brian, and Ken.

That was twenty-two years ago. Jeff has gone on to serve youth in his church and has recently gone on a short-term missions trip. Hua, Brian, and Ken continue to pass on their lives through new spiritual generations.

Last month, at forty-three years old, Craig went home to be with the Lord after a rough battle with cancer. He didn't have a long life, but he had a successful one. He left behind a wife and two young children. He also left behind a continuing spiritual heritage that is still making an impact for the kingdom of God.

4c. How does thinking in terms of three to four generations affect the way we minister (teach, act, prepare, train) compared to anticipating only one or two generations?

POWER IN THE GENERATIONAL CONCEPT

Consider the diagram at right, in which an addition model is compared to a multiplication-doubling model.

5a. Compare the two models at three years, at twelve years, and at thirty-three years. What observations do you make in comparing the two models?

The Multiplication Principle

End of Year	Daily Addition Model	Annual Multiplication
0	1	1
1	365	2
2	730	4
3	1,095	8
4	1,460	16
5	1,825	32
6	2,190	64
7	2,555	128
8	2,920	256
9	3,285	512
10	3,650	1,024
11	4,015	2,048
12	4,380	4,096
13	4,745	8,192
14	5,110	16,384
15	5,475	32,768
20	7,300	1,048,576
25	9,125	33,554,432
30	10,950	1,073,741,824
33	12,045	8,589,934,5921

5b. What are the liabilities and benefits of each?

5c. How would an illustration like this one relate to your spiritual multiplication?

5d. Why hasn't this multiplication principle worked already?

SUMMARY

6. What significance does the concept of spiritual generations have for you personally?

7. What is one practical step you can take to apply what you have learned in this study?

Multiple, continuous links hold a chain together. Each person can be a link in a spiritual chain that reaches into the future. The chain creates a legacy of spiritual decedents allowing "one to become a thousand" and "a little one, a mighty nation."

Motivation: For a Lifetime of Disciplemaking

by Jim White

SEEING AN EXAMPLE, OBSERVING the need, achieving success—all this can motivate us in the work of helping others grow as disciples.

But better motivations are:

- the love of God filling our heart
- our own desire to grow

- embracing God's Word in our mind
- our longing to see God glorified

Looking back on my days of child rearing, I can see that some things I designed to motivate my children had exactly the opposite effect. Our attempts to motivate others in the Christian life can be just as ineffective. We can teach and train them, but only the Holy Spirit can truly motivate them to a lifetime of discipleship and disciplemaking.

We need motivation. It's too easy to sit in our offices and homes doing everything we can in life except the hard work of disciplemaking.

But even once we have it, we can lose our motivation. Many people who were motivated early in life to be disciplemakers aren't motivated now.

A man who led the campus ministry I was involved in as a university student impressed me as one of the most spiritual men I ever met. But years later he told me he was convinced nothing was important in his life except television and sex. One of the other men who was on the same disciplemaking team is now a university teacher in a foreign country, where he leads the Communist party on his campus.

Paul wrote near the end of his life that his disciple Demas had deserted him "because he loved this world" (2 Timothy 4:10). And Jesus said that in the last times, "most people's love will grow cold" (Matthew 24:12). You're probably motivated to be an instrument in God's hands in the lives of others, but from Jesus' words, we see that the world is a deep-freeze that can numb your desire. All of Satan's schemes are designed to keep us from carrying out a lifetime of disciplemaking.

What will motivate us to continue?

AN EXAMPLE

Seeing someone else make disciples is one motivation. Albert Schweitzer said that setting an example is not the main means of influencing another, but the only means. I wouldn't say it quite that strongly, but it is a powerful means.

I remember hearing Billy Graham at a meeting in the Cotton Bowl in Dallas in 1953. I'd just attended a weeklong Navigator conference where we heard Dawson Trotman speak throughout the week. I had been greatly touched by Daws's love for people.

After Billy Graham concluded his message and gave the invitation for people to come forward, I spotted Daws down on the field in a white cowboy outfit. He was like a field general, confidently directing the people to the counselors ready to help them. I was sitting on the fifty-yard line, about sixty rows up, watching him work.

Then I saw him glance at the sidelines where an elderly lady was sitting in a wheelchair, apparently waiting on someone. Daws called for an assistant to take over his job, and he went over to her, took her hand, then reached in his pocket and pulled out a New Testament. He knelt beside her, read a few verses of Scripture, and prayed with her. Then he got up, patted her on the hand, and returned to the field to resume his job. That example has stayed with me ever since to remind me what it means to have a heart for people.

When I was a high school senior, a university student who had preached at our church called me up from his university, which was hundreds of miles from my home. He asked me to come with him on a weekend ministry trip to a church just an hour north of his university. I asked how I would get there, and he said he would come get me.

So after his Friday afternoon classes, he drove to my home and got there after midnight. Early the next morning we left on the drive to the church, and all weekend I watched him minister to people. He drove me back home Sunday night, arriving about 1 o'clock in the morning. I was sleeping on the way so I could get up and go to school the next morning. He drove the rest of the night to get back to the university in time for his classes.

He drove a total of eighteen hours that weekend, instead of only two, just so he could spend time with me in the car traveling, and let me watch him minister to people. I'll never forget that. Examples really do motivate.

SEEING NEEDS

Years ago a man old enough to be my father came up to me and said he wanted to know how to get some discipleship help in his life. I hemmed and hawed, because in our ministry we were working only with college students, and I didn't know anyone else who could help him. But he was persistent, and I saw the tremendous hunger and desire he had.

So for about six months I got up at 4:30 every Monday morning and drove about an hour to his house to spend time with him and another man. I did it simply because of his hunger, the need he expressed in his life.

SUCCESS

For twelve years, my wife and I had as many as seven young men and women at a time living in our home to receive training from us. My main ministry was simply giving myself to them. These men and women have gone on to serve ministries not only in the United States but also in Austria, Canada, Argentina, Korea, New Zealand, the Netherlands, the Philippines, and Nigeria. It's so exciting for my wife and me to think how it really does pay to share life and home with others.

Seeing an example, seeing the needs, and seeing success—these can all motivate us. But I believe none of these is adequate. All can fail us. If they're our only motivation, the white heat of devotion to disciplemaking will wane.

HEARTS FLOODED WITH GOD'S LOVE

This may be the most important motivation of all. Paul wrote, "For Christ's love compels us, because we are convinced that one died for all" (2 Corinthians 5:14).

It's been said that no one can love another until he first has been loved himself. If each of us knew how much God really loves us, we would be enraptured with joy and would never know another insecure moment. We'd be truly free to love others.

Our problem is that, on our own, we don't have that overwhelming sense of how much God loves us. But God has done something about this, as we see in Romans 5:3-5:

> We can rejoice, too, when we run into problems and trials, for we know that they are good for us—they help us learn to be patient. And patience develops strength of character in us and helps us trust God more each time we use it, until finally our hope and faith are strong and steady.
>
> Then we are able to hold our heads high no matter what happens, and know that all is well. For we know how dearly God loves us, and we feel this warm love everywhere within us because God has given us the Holy Spirit to fill our hearts with his love. (TLB)

The Holy Spirit must reveal to us how much God loves us. Then our insecurities will begin to fade, and we can freely let our lives overflow to other people.

DESIRE TO GROW OURSELVES

Paul wrote to the Romans, "I long to see you so that I may impart to you some spiritual gift to make you strong—that is, that you and I may be mutually encouraged by each other's faith" (Romans 1:11-12).

Paul longed to be personally involved in building up people as disciples, but this would also be for his own growth and encouragement. I doubt that the person who thinks he has everything packaged for establishing and equipping disciples will ever continue in a lifetime of disciplemaking. But someone who wants to grow knows he must listen and learn.

GOD'S WORD BURNING IN OUR HEARTS

Sooner or later, all of us will go through tough times. Jeremiah was going through such a time as recorded in Jeremiah 20:7-9, and he responded this way: "I am ridiculed all day long; everyone mocks me. Whenever I speak, I cry out proclaiming violence and destruction. So the word of the Lord has brought me insult and reproach all day long. But if I say, 'I will not mention him or speak any more in his name, his word is in my heart like a burning fire.'"

The word of God burning in our hearts will keep us going.

I know a man named Hubert Mitchell who several years ago completed memorizing the entire New Testament. As a former missionary in his sixties, he spent his days in downtown Chicago, going from office building to office building. Inside, he would ask secretaries if he could have five minutes with their boss to talk about a personal matter. Frequently, he'd be ushered into the boss's office, and he would say, "I only have five minutes, but I want to ask you, did you read your Bible before you came to work this morning?"

The boss would look at him as if he were crazy, and say, "No."

Hubert would smile and answer, "Sir, you sure missed a blessing, didn't you? I'd just like to share with you what God spoke about to me in the Bible this morning." He would open a New Testament and hand it to the boss, and say, "Let's start right here." Then Hubert would sit back and start quoting it word-for-word.

The boss would listen, amazed. After five minutes, Hubert would say, "My time's up and I've got to go. Wasn't that a blessing?" On many occasions, the boss would ask him to stay longer, and they'd talk.

Hubert Mitchell led men to Christ all over downtown Chicago that way, because God's Word was burning in his heart.

DESIRE TO SEE GOD GLORIFIED

This can be tricky because, as one Christian leader told me several years ago, there's so much in Christian leadership that caters to personality needs in the leader's life that it's hard for him to know what his motives are.

We can get into all kinds of introspection and psychological confusion by spending too much time wondering about our motives. But at some point early in the game we need to settle the matter: "God, I'm going to do this for your glory as best I know how. If I ever start doing it for my glory, will you tap me on the shoulder before I go too far?"

When others are looking to you for leadership, if you're not careful you can begin to let that meet a security need in your life. If you're building disciples who will lean on Christ and not on you, then you know your motive is God's glory—though there may be a time when they must lean on you to a certain degree.

A few years ago, in a press conference following a ceremony where Corrie ten Boom was given an honorary degree, one of the reporters asked her if it was difficult remaining humble while hearing so much acclaim. She replied immediately, "Young man, when Jesus Christ rode into Jerusalem on Palm Sunday on the back of a donkey, and everyone was waving palm branches and throwing garments in the road and singing praises, do you think that for one moment it ever entered the head of that donkey that any of that was for him?"

She continued, "If I can be the donkey on which Jesus Christ rides in His glory, I give Him all the praise and all the honor."

Our hearts should be clear about doing what we do because we want Christ to be glorified.

These are the right motivations that will keep us in disciplemaking over the years: God's love, the desire in our own hearts to keep growing, God's word burning within us, and a sincere desire to see God glorified.

What can take away our motivation? One thing that will is becoming system-centered rather than God-centered. There's a fine line here. I believe a lot of people aren't making disciples because they don't have a system and they don't know what to do. But if you take structure too far, God gets pushed out of the picture.

That's what happened to the Pharisees. They memorized the Scriptures, but there was no passion coming from their lives, and the disciples they made were disciples of a system rather than disciples of God. Jesus said, "They worship me in vain; their teachings are but rules taught by men" (Mark 7:7).

Presbyterian pastor and author Richard Halverson was asked what he would say if he could give only one piece of advice to someone going into the Christian ministry. He answered, "Don't get professional. There's no vocation in the world where it's easier to become a stuffed shirt than the Christian ministry."

Jesus warned us about another crippler of our motivation in Mark 4:19: "the worries of this life" that come in and choke God's Word and make it unfruitful. This anxiety means we're self-conscious rather than God-conscious or others-conscious.

I've found as my responsibilities increased over the years that one of the greatest temptations keeping me from giving myself to other people at opportune moments is my preoccupation with a decision I need to make or a problem I need to solve. But God's Word tells us to cast our anxieties on Him.

Lust will also derail us. Before I moved to Africa in 1967, a man came up to me at a Navigator conference with lines in his face disclosing years of physical and emotional hardship. He said he had been around Dawson Trotman and other Navigators in the war years, but then began running out on his wife and giving himself to money and possessions. He later lost his wife and his health. He said his last twenty years had been hell.

His lust had knocked him out of a life of disciplemaking. I'll never forget the look on his face.

Don't let something like that happen to you. Ask God to let His Holy Spirit flood your heart with His love, to show you how much He loves you so you can turn to others and love them.

And make this vow to Him: "Lord, I know I'm human and I'll break this vow before tomorrow morning without your grace. But to the best of my ability for the rest of my life, I will do what I can for your glory."

Ask the Lord also to help you respond in faith to His Word, with excitement and obedience.

And finally, ask God to send someone or some experience to get your attention whenever you begin to veer off course, so you can correct yourself before it's too late.

I can't think of a better prayer than this: "Lord, on the day You return or on the day You take me home, may there never have been a day in my life when I loved You more or was obeying You more quickly than on that last day."[1]

QUESTIONS FOR REFLECTION

1. As you review the possible motivations listed in this article, which ones seem to influence you the most?
2. Which ones do you think would keep you discipling for a lifetime? Why?

▶ TIPS FOR DISCIPLING

Discipling over the Long Haul

by Francisco Arzadon IV

I discipled Ricky back in our college days. We met every week for Bible study and one-to-one counseling and training. As he got busy during his senior year, he slowly drifted away from such intense involvement. But once in a while we bumped into each other and would briefly share what was happening in our lives. He later invited me to help prepare for his wedding, and when he opened a food business, I became an occasional customer. One day, he decided to invest heavily in his business. Since that time, he and his wife have been consulting me about the decisions they face. I feel as if we're back to the good old days of really being involved in one another's lives.

From my experience with Ricky and others I've discipled, I've learned the value of maintaining an open hand. After building basic biblical foundations in their lives, we should give our disciples enough space to decide for themselves what level of relationship they need from us. That level may change often through the years.

One common pitfall among disciplers is the tendency to constantly exert control. We can become overbearing in our efforts to keep people "on track." Such a relationship can be stifling and offensive, so that as soon as the people we disciple can escape our control, they will. As disciplers, we can learn from the farmer who plants the seed, then patiently waits for his crop to grow and bear fruit. Sometimes that fruit comes years after discipling—if we keep an open hand.

The following are some principles in maintaining an "open hand relationship."

See your discipling relationship as long term. This will remove the pressure to dump too much on a young disciple in a short time.

Be sensitive. Take note of the level of spiritual hunger in the person you're discipling. Listen to him, and learn what he is excited about. Don't give him more than he is eager to receive.

Don't be disappointed. When someone doesn't meet your expectations, give him the freedom to grow at his own pace.

Become a resource person. Maintain an open-ended relationship. Stay in touch even after your formal discipling relationship ends.

Be there for critical moments. Use natural entry points in his life (wedding, change of career, first baby, death in the family, and so forth).

Keep on praying. Ask God to make your disciple what God wants him to be.[2]

DISCIPLING RESOURCES

A VARIETY OF MATERIALS are available to use for discipling others. You can use Bible studies and books to help new believers understand how to live out their new relationships with Christ. We recommend, however, that you personally disciple others in the context of looking at the Scriptures firsthand. Helping others discover truth from God's Word not only gives them truth but also demonstrates the importance of Scripture in their lives.

Disciples depend on the Word of God as their primary source of spiritual food. By taking new believers directly to the Bible to explain spiritual truth, we demonstrate that "man does not live on bread alone but on every word that comes from the mouth of the LORD" (Deuteronomy 8:3).

We suggest the following materials for use in discipling others. These are produced by NavPress. Each of these materials covers a similar range of topics but in differing formats. We've arranged them in order of increasing difficulty or complexity.

Studies in Christian Living

This six-book series contains three to four short lessons in each book. Participants can do the question-and-answer format together or prepare in advance.

Growing in Christ

This one book of twelve lessons has a simple Q & A style and includes a primary verse for each lesson. It also includes a key verse to memorize along with the lesson.

Design for Discipleship

This seven-book series covers a wide range of topics. Use it sequentially or as separate studies. A general progression through the series moves from basic topics to more in-depth issues. Preparing for this series requires an hour or more of study.

The 2:7 In God's Family Series

This three-book series is the most complex of the list. It combines Bible study with other spiritual disciplines, such as devotional life, Scripture memory, and witnessing. All three books are built around The Navigators' "Wheel" illustration. This is more of a training series and requires homework and accountability.

Foundations for Christian Living

This eight-book series focuses on key themes for rooting your life in Christ. These studies are unique in that they develop simultaneously on two tracks: Bible study and developing community in a small group.

------◆------

Other materials are available from other publishers. The discipler needs to be familiar with the material to confidently lead others. As the discipler becomes more skilled, he or she will need to build a greater resource list. Skilled disciplers fit the material to the person rather than forcing the person into the materials.

WHO'S ON YOUR HEART FOR HEAVEN?

LIST PEOPLE IN YOUR networks whom God has placed on your heart for heaven. These are people you know who you desire to come to faith in Christ. List those of other group members so you can pray for them as well. You'll be able to share what God is doing in their lives as the course progresses. During the duration of the course, you may add to these names.

Group Member: _____   Group Member: _____
Names: _____   Names: _____
_____   _____
_____   _____
_____   _____

Group Member: _____   Group Member: _____
Names: _____   Names: _____
_____   _____
_____   _____
_____   _____

Group Member: _____   Group Member: _____
Names: _____   Names: _____
_____   _____
_____   _____
_____   _____

Group Member: _____   Group Member: _____
Names: _____   Names: _____
_____   _____
_____   _____
_____   _____

POTENTIAL DISCIPLES LIST

RECORD THE NAMES OF people that each group member is considering inviting into a discipling context. This list can be modified each week. It can also serve as a prayer list during the course.

Group Member:_____   Group Member: _____
Potential Disciples: _____   Potential Disciples: _____
_____   _____
_____   _____
_____   _____

Group Member:_____   Group Member: _____
Potential Disciples: _____   Potential Disciples: _____
_____   _____
_____   _____
_____   _____

Group Member:_____   Group Member: _____
Potential Disciples: _____   Potential Disciples: _____
_____   _____
_____   _____
_____   _____

Group Member:_____   Group Member: _____
Potential Disciples: _____   Potential Disciples: _____
_____   _____
_____   _____
_____   _____

THE HAND ILLUSTRATION

GETTING A GRASP ON THE WORD OF GOD

Here is a "pass-on-able" illustration you can use when you study with your group.

Label each finger: hear, read, and so on. Here are percentages of recall:

Hear	5-10%
Read	20-30%
Study	60-75%
Memorize	100%
Meditate	Unlimited

Emphasize meditation as

- essential to grasping something as thumb is to fingers
- and the key to getting something out of the other four.

Grasp your Bible with an increasing number of fingers, giving you additional strength.

ADDITIONAL READING

Bailey, Mark. *To Follow Him: The Seven Marks of Discipleship.* Portland, Ore., Multnomah, 1997.

Barna, George. *Growing True Disciples: New Strategies for Producing Genuine Follower of Christ.* Colorado Springs, Colo., Waterbrook Press, 2001.

Bennett, Ron. *Intentional Disciplemaking: Cultivating Maturity in the Local Church.* Colorado Springs, Colo., NavPress, 2000.

Coleman, Robert. *The Master Plan of Evangelism.* Westwood, N.J.: Revell, 1963.

Eims, LeRoy. *The Lost Art of Disciplemaking.* Grand Rapids, Mich., Zondervan, 1978.

Hettinga, Jan. *Follow Me.* Colorado Springs, Colo., NavPress, 1996.

Hodges, Herb. *Tally Ho the Fox.* Memphis, Tenn., Spiritual Life Ministries, 2000.

Petersen, Jim. *Lifestyle Discipleship: The Challenge of Following Christ in Today's World.* Colorado Springs, Colo., NavPress, 1993.

Rabey, Steve. *Side by Side: Disciplemaking for a New Generation.* Colorado Springs, Colo., NavPress, 2000.

Willard, Dallas. *The Divine Conspiracy: Rediscovering Our Hidden Life in God.* San Francisco, HarperCollins, 1998.

Mentoring/Coaching
Paul D. Stanley and J. Robert Clinton. *Connecting: The Mentoring Relationships You Need to Succeed in Life.* Colorado Spring, Colo., NavPress, 1992.

Spiritual Disciplines
Bridges, Jerry. *Transforming Grace: Living Confidently in God's Unfailing Love.* Colorado Springs, Colo., NavPress, 1993.

Foster, Richard. *Celebration of Discipline: The Path to Spiritual Growth.* San Francisco, Harper, 1998.

Whitney, Donald. *Spiritual Disciplines for the Christian Life.* Colorado Springs, Colo., NavPress, 1991.

Willard, Dallas. *The Spirit of the Disciplines: Understanding How God Changes Lives.* San Francisco, HarperCollins, 1991.

Learning Environment
Donahue, Bill. *Leading Life Changing Small Groups.* Grand Rapids, Mich., Zondervan, 1996.

McBride, Neal. *How to Build a Small Groups Ministry.* Colorado Springs, Colo., NavPress, 1994.

NOTES

SESSION 1: THE DISCIPLING VISION
1. Lee Brase, "Who Me? Make Disciples?" *Discipleship Journal* 60, November/December 1990, p. 40
2. Reprinted from Robert D. Foster, *The Navigator* (Colorado Springs, Colo., 1983), pp. 113-116.
3. From Daryl Donovan, "In Pursuit of Disciples," *Discipleship Journal* 111, May/June 1999, p. 89.

SESSION 2: THE GREAT COMMISSION
1. Compilation of notes from Desmond Alexander, et al., *The New Dictionary of Biblical Theology* (Downers Grove, Ill.: InterVarsity, 2001), pp. 262-273; and *The Open Bible, New Living Translation* (Nashville, Tenn.: Thomas Nelson, 1998), p. 1228.
2. Lynn Austin, "Mentoring Toward Maturity," *Discipleship Journal* 92, March/April 1996.
3. Karen H. Whiting, "Mentoring New Disciplers," *Discipleship Journal* 121.

SESSION 3: DESCRIPTION OF A DISCIPLE
1. Dallas Willard, *The Divine Conspiracy* (New York: HarperCollins, 1998), pp. 299-300.
2. George Barna, *Growing True Disciples* (Colorado Springs, Colo.: WaterBrook Press, 2001), p. 20.
3. Ron E. Bennett, *Intentional Disciplemaking* (Colorado Springs, Colo.: NavPress, 2001).
4. Becky Brodin, "Finding the Right Person to Disciple," *Discipleship Journal* 115, January/February 2000, p. 20.

SESSION 4: MINISTERING LIFE-TO-LIFE
1. Paul exhorted the Corinthians to follow him not primarily by following his personal example but by following his "way of life in Christ" which he taught "everywhere in every church" (1 Corinthians 4:16-17). The Corinthians were to follow Paul's example by heeding his counsel to do all for the glory of God without causing offense (1 Corinthians 11:1; compare 1 Corinthians 10:23-33). In Ephesians 5:1, the command to be imitators is again linked with the previous series of commands, especially that of forgiveness (Ephesians 4:25-32). The image of children obedient to parents is common where the thought of imitation as obedience is primary (1 Corinthians 4:14-16; Ephesians 5:1). WORDSearch CD-ROM (Austin, Tex.: iExalt Electronic Publishing, 1987).
2. Kenneth Wuest points out that the Greek word means to follow a person so closely that one is always by the person's side, conforming his life to the person. "The Pastoral Epistles," *Word Studies in the Greek New Testament* (Grand Rapids, Mich.: Eerdmans, 1961), p. 148.
3. William Barclay, *The Daily Study Bible* (Louisville, Ky.: Westminster/John Knox Press, 1993), pp. 225.
4. Jack Griffin, "Guidelines and Checklist for the One-to-One Discipler," *Discipleship Journal* 15, p. 88. These pointers on one-to-one discipling are from the booklet "Man to Man: How to Do Individual Disciplemaking" by Jack Griffin, who began the Navigator ministry in Australia with his wife, May, in the 1960s.

Session 5: Follow Me

1. Quoted in Jan Hettinga, *Follow Me: Experience the Loving Leadership of Jesus* (Colorado Springs, Colo.: NavPress, 1996), pp. 13-14.

2. Gordon MacDonald, "Questions I'd Ask Before Following Jesus," *Discipleship Journal* 100, pp. 89-92.

Session 6: Parental Prayer

1. J. Oswald Sanders, "The Prayers of a Leader," *Discipleship Journal* 41, pp. 36-37. Adapted from *Spiritual Leadership,* Copyright 1967, 1980, Moody Bible Institute of Chicago, Moody Press.

2. Adapted from Alice Fryling, *Disciplemakers' Handbook* (Downers Grove, Ill.: InterVarsity, 1989), p. 48.

Session 7: Faith and the Promises of God

1. Skip Gray, "Living by Promises," *Discipleship Journal* 31.

Session 8: Habits of the Heart

1. Richard Foster, *The Celebration of Discipline* (New York: HarperCollins, 1988), p. 6.

2. From R. Paul Stevens, *The Complete Book of Everyday Christianity* on WORDSearch CD-ROM (Austin, Tex.: iExalt Electronic Publishing, 1987).

3. Beth Moore, *Breaking Free* (Nashville, Tenn.: LifeWay Press, 1999), p. 69.

4. Donald Whitney, *Spiritual Disciplines for the Christian Life* (Colorado Springs, Colo.: NavPress, 1997), pp. 13-18.

5. From Jerry Bridges, "How to Develop Learners, Not Legalists," *Disicpleship Journal* 54, p. 74.

6. Alan Andrews, U.S. Director of The Navigators, from an e-mail to staff, Spring 2002.

Session 9: The Process of Disciplemaking

1. Bill Hull, *Jesus Christ Disciple Maker* (Westwood, N.J.: Revell, 1990).

2. Robert N. Nielsen, "We're in This Together," *Discipleship Journal* 67, pp. 42-43.

3. Rebecca Livermore, "Ways to Help an Apathetic Disciple," *Discipleship Journal* 109, p. 87.

Session 10: The Importance of the Word

1. Joni Eareckson Tada, "Speaking God's Language," *Discipleship Journal* 111, p. 56.

Session 11: The Value of Each Individual

1. C. S. Lewis, *Mere Christianity* (Grand Rapids, Mich.: Zondervan, 2001), p. 97.

2. Lorne Sanny, "The Importance of Every Individual," *Discipleship Journal* 2, March 1981, pp. 24-25.

3. Kathy Kelly, "Don't Give Up Yet," *Discipleship Journal* 112, p. 20.

Session 12: Spiritual Generations

1. Jim White, "Motivation: For a Lifetime of Disciplemaking," *Discipleship Journal* 3, Spring 1981.

2. Francisco Arzadon IV, "Discipling over the Long Haul," *Discipleship Journal* 99, p. 87.

CDM™

CHURCH DISCIPLESHIP MINISTRY

CDM is a mission of The Navigators that focuses on helping churches become more intentional in discipleship and outreach. CDM staff help pastors and church leaders develop an effective and personalized approach to accomplishing the Great Commission.

Through a nationwide network of staff, CDM works alongside the local church to build a strong structure for disciplemaking—one that is intentional. Six critical areas are core to an Intentional Disciplemaking Church:

- Mission

- Spiritual Maturity

- Outreach

- Leadership

- Small Groups

- Life to Life

CDM offers seminars, materials, and coaching in these six areas for those interested in becoming an Intentional Disciplemaking Church. See our web page for further information on how CDM can help you.

www.navigators.org/cdm
or email to cdm@navigators.org
or call our CDM Office at (719) 598-1212
or write to PO Box 6000, Colorado Springs, CO 80934

DISCIPLESHIP RESOURCES FROM CHURCH DISCIPLESHIP MINISTRY (CDM) AND NAVPRESS.

Opening the Door

Opening the Door is a user-friendly discipleship guide full of tips on preparation, being an effective facilitator, and recruiting new seekers. Includes Discovery Guide worksheets that can be photocopied for multiple use.

The Navigators   978-1-57683-346-9

Intentional Disciplemaking:
Cultivating Spiritual Maturity in the Local Church

How does a church make disciples? They're developed through intentional planning and the effort of a community of believers. Here's help for churches that want to make disciples—on purpose.

The Navigators   978-1-57683-262-2

Jesus: The Way   **Jesus: The Truth**   **Jesus: The Life**
The Navigators   *The Navigators*   *The Navigators*
978-1-57683-349-0   978-1-57683-707-8   978-1-57683-708-5

New from the Church Discipleship Ministry team at the Navigators comes a new Bible study series on the life and supremacy of Jesus Christ. An excellent resource for new and growing believers, the BEGINNING THE WALK series focuses on readers' fundamental relationship with Jesus rather than technical details of how to study or interpret the Bible.

To order copies, call NavPress at 1-800-366-7788 or log on to www.navpress.com.

NAVPRESS
Discipleship Inside Out™